Clinical Depression

The Overlooked and Insidious Nemesis Plaguing ADHD Children

Paul Lavin

UNIVERSITY PRESS OF AMERICA,® INC.

Lanham • Boulder • New York • Toronto • Plymouth, UK

Copyright © 2008 by
University Press of America,® Inc.
4501 Forbes Boulevard
Suite 200
Lanham, Maryland 20706
UPA Acquisitions Department (301) 459-3366

Estover Road
Plymouth PL6 7PY
United Kingdom

Library of Congress Control Number: 2007933967
ISBN-13: 978-0-7618-3863-0 (paperback : alk. paper)
ISBN-10: 0-7618-3863-5 (paperback : alk. paper)

∞™ The paper used in this publication meets the minimum
requirements of American National Standard for Information
Sciences—Permanence of Paper for Printed Library Materials,
ANSI Z39.48—1984

Contents

Chapter One

Introduction

There are three characteristics of ADHD children, which interfere with their ability to function at home, at school, and in the community.[1] First, ADHD children often have poor control of their bodies. Their hands, arms, feet, and legs are in constant motion. Try as they might, they have marked difficulty keeping such movement within acceptable boundaries. Violating the personal space of other people is all too common. Excessive fingering, touching, flopping about, stamping, and tapping create sounds, sights, and distractions that are extremely annoying to adults and peers alike. Moreover, the inadvertent accidents and disruptions that these cause can also be most unsettling to those around them.

Second, ADHD children have marked difficulty sustaining concentration and completing assigned tasks. Constant looking about, becoming easily distracted by extraneous sounds, sights, and smells, and the failure to follow instructions and to complete assignments occur repeatedly. This leads to poor grades, gross underachievement, and the failure to develop his or her intellectual potential.

Third, ADHD children often behave impulsively. They engage in disorganized, disruptive, and even antisocial actions without any semblance of forethought or planning. Like an airplane on automatic pilot, they seem to be unable to direct or control their actions so that a crash course can be avoided. Rather, they virtually propel themselves into the environment, which often produces devastating results for them and those persons who just happen to be within the surrounding area. When such behavior occurs, the youngster appears bewildered as to why he or she acted in this manner. When asked why he or she behaved so poorly, a satisfactory explanation cannot be given. Rather, "I don't know" answers usually accompany such inquiries. And the truth of the matter is that ADHD children do not know why they act as they do. They, like those who live and work with them, are befuddled by the reasons of their errant actions.

It is important to note that the diagnosis of ADHD is usually made by the age of seven years.[2] This means that the preceding behaviors have occurred for most of the young child's life, during his or her most formidable years of personality development. It is obvious that throughout this period of time, the youngster's poor self-control and impulsivity would have become of marked concern to parents, teachers, and peers. In fact, it is highly likely that the ADHD child would have received considerable negative criticism for his or her actions. Parents and educators are quite likely to become frustrated with the youngster. Their rational explanations, well intentioned reprimands, and encouragement will appear to have fallen on deaf ears. It is easy, therefore, to view the child's behavior as being willful or just plain stubborn. As a result, a flood of complaints, criticisms, and admonitions can be heaped upon the youngster, who again, is in the most malleable years upon which the foundation of his or her personality is built.

The preceding, although not intended to be so, can have a devastating impact on the ADHD child's mental health. The youngster can quickly conclude that he or she "is not liked" by the most important adults in his or her life. Moreover, complaining peers can add to this perception of not being liked as well.

As noted earlier, adults and ADHD children alike are confused and bewildered as to why such counterproductive behavior continues in the face of such criticism. ADHD youngsters don't really intentionally choose to be annoying. They, too, want the respect, love, and friendship of those around them. Unfortunately, they have neither the insight nor capability in order to achieve this goal. It is up to parents, teachers, and mental health professionals to train them in order to bring this about. How can a developing child build the rudiments of a positive self-concept unless the proper conditions are established to do so? How can the ADHD youngster develop confidence in him or herself unless he or she believes that his or her efforts can and will lead to success? ADHD children who live in a sea of criticism and admonitions are unlikely to develop a positive view of themselves or other people. Rather than expect to succeed, they will anticipate failure, believing that they can do little, if anything, to control their destiny.

The preceding, in effect, is the way depressed persons think and behave. Like a cat on a hot tin roof, they jump from one excuse to another rather than accept responsibility for their actions. Their interior disposition is one of hopelessness, even though they might act-out or engage in various forms of oppositional behavior. And it is this hopelessness that must be addressed and overcome if progress is to occur. This is partially true for ADHD children who have been plummeted with the negative reactions of others accompanied by repeated failure at home and school. Unless they can learn to change their counterproductive views about themselves, other people, and life itself, future success is likely to continue to escape them.

In order to alter this course, the ADHD child must learn to replace the hopelessness with hopefulness. The insidious and often unrecognized depression that blocks this must be addressed and put to rest. This, in essence, is what this book is all about. Its purpose is to provide parents, teachers, and mental health professionals with a conceptual and practical framework for identifying and correcting this emotional virus, which can undermine even the most well-designed and implemented therapeutic and educational program.

NOTES

1. Paul Lavin and Kathryn Lavin, *A Comprehensive Guide for Parenting the ADHD Child*. (Baltimore, MD: Publish America, 2005), 11–16.

2. American Psychiatric Association, *Quick Reference to the Diagnostic Criteria from. DSM-IV*. (Washington, DC: American Psychiatric Association, 1994), 63–65.

Chapter Two

ADHD and Depression:
Its Prevalence and Symptoms

The research indicates that 10 to 30 percent of ADHD children are diagnosed as being clinically depressed.[1] Several well-conducted studies have shown that becoming depressed during the course of their development is as much as three times greater for ADHD youngsters than their peers.[2] Moreover, this depression does not just go away with the passage of time. Studies show that 47 percent of adults with ADHD suffer from depression as well.[3] Although ADHD might be the precursor for this disorder, the preceding would suggest that the occurrence of depression actually increases with age. Further, it would appear that this depression is either unrecognized or unsuccessfully treated during the ADHD child's most formative years.

It is this author's contention that depression is much more prevalent than statistics indicate. The above only identifies those youngsters who are diagnosed as being clinical depressed by a physician or mental health professional. The data does not necessarily take into account those ADHD young people who live in a discouraged and dispirited state that continues from one day to the next. The daily bombardment of peer rejection, criticism, and ongoing unsatisfactory performance at home and school can only create a perpetual condition of sadness, which can gradually crush what little self-esteem that exists in the child's fragile psyche.

It is of interest to note that nearly half of ADHD children, particularly boys, are diagnosed with Oppositional Defiant Disorder (e.g. negative, hostile, defiant behavior) and about 40 percent are diagnosed with Conduct Disorder (e.g. aggression toward others, destruction of property, theft, serious rule violations, etc.).[4] These statistics exceed those of ADHD children who are diagnosed with anxiety or depression. It is this author's belief that depression is the "sleeper," which often is overlooked when the preceding diagnoses are

4

made. Oppositional Defiant and Conduct Disorder are often identified long after the diagnosis of ADHD is made. In essence, we might say that Oppositional Defiant and Conduct Disorder "grow out" of the child's ADHD. Attention Deficit Hyperactivity Disorder (ADHD) is the root, which if not recognized and properly attended to, can lead to major behavioral problems as the child passes from one developmental stage to the next.

It is this author's view that young people, who become defiant and antisocial, are often reacting to feelings of demoralization, which become more frequent and intense over time. This particularly makes sense if we consider that these youngsters often have a long history of failure at home, school, and in the community. As a result, they are not only distrustful of adults, but they develop a lack of confidence and a strong sense of inferiority in comparison to their better-prepared age mates.[5] Their failure to master those developmental tasks, which are typically accomplished by their peers, is a constant affirmation that they just don't measure up to others.[6]

It is no surprise that some children engage in defiant and antisocial behavior as a reaction to this. Such behavior can be symptomatic of a chronic "low grade" depression or demoralization that has slowly destroyed the child's self-confidence and any hope of achieving successfully. This underlying negative emotional malaise and hopelessness can virtually infect and compromise the healthy growth of his or her personality.

As indicated previously, this author believes that the number of ADHD children suffering with depression is much more pervasive than indicated by current statistics. And unless this is identified and treated accordingly, it may undermine our efforts to treat the precursor, which leads to this in the first place—Attention Deficit Hyperactivity Disorder.

It should be kept in mind that children do not choose to be afflicted with ADHD. Rather, it is inherited or acquired by factors outside of their control. As a result, ADHD children can become very frustrated and resentful toward those who treat them as if they were engaging in willful behavior. Again, ADHD youngsters do not wish this disorder on themselves. This must be seriously taken into account in working with them. Empathizing with their plight is a critical first step in helping them to cope with this problem. This will be addressed in a chapter to follow.

What are the symptoms of depression? How do depressed children behave? The answers to these questions are important in determining whether ADHD children are depressed and whether this depression is interfering with their ability to function. It should first be pointed out that depression is a feeling, not a behavior. Depressed persons experience a feeling of intense sadness, which seldom abates. A sad child is one whose attention is inwardly focused. In other words, the child constantly ruminates or thinks about his or her problems, frustrations, anxieties, or other emotionally laden issues that plague him or her. The youngster often appears to be in another world and has a far away look in his or her eyes. Because the child is so inwardly focused, he or she is hardly aware of what is transpiring in the surrounding environment.

Depression robs the child of his or her vitality, leaving very little energy for facing and coping with the challenges of everyday living. It is an emotional siphon that drains away the child's inner resources. It is no wonder that depression is one of the leading causes for poor school performance. Beside withdrawal, behaviors characteristic of depression include learning difficulties, acting-out, antisocial activity, drug and alcohol abuse, promiscuity, phobias, and sleeping and eating problems (too little or too much of either). In the extreme, depressed persons may engage in excessive risk taking, showing little concerns for life and limb. They may become violent and suicidal.

It is important to keep in mind that different age groups manifest the characteristics of depression in different ways. The younger the child, the less likely it is that he or she will be able to recognize his or her feelings and use words to describe these or the thoughts associated with them. Young children tend to act-out, rather than talk about emotions, particularly if these are negative in nature.

With regard to the preceding, let's examine symptoms that might be indicative of depression with children in the first five or six years of life, which are the most formative in the development of the youngster's self-concept.[7,8] Common characteristics of this age period are: a detached far away look in his or her eyes, periodic displays of aggression and anger, and irritability and moodiness. Depressed children may experience headaches, stomachaches, nausea, cramps, bed-wetting, too much or too little sleep, nightmares, and night terrors. Other characteristics include hitting and fighting with peers, lying, and stealing. Withdrawal and loss of interest in activities that were once enjoyed and a morbid preoccupation with death or dying may occur. Depression children may become more prone to accidents and injuries. They may vacillate between listlessness and hyper-out-of-control behavior. Marked difficulty separating from parents, which may be accomplished by temper outbursts and crying are quite common as well.

Needless to say the characteristics of childhood depression are quite numerous. The failure to recognize and treat these in the child's most formative years increases the likelihood that they will continue and worsen over the course of time. While ADHD children may not exhibit the more blatant signs of depression, any one or combination of the less significant symptoms could be indicative that this may be interfering with the youngster's ability to function. Depressed children lose their motivation. They lack the desire to make those efforts needed to cope with and master the many problems associated with their ADHD, and they have little or no confidence in their ability to perform successfully. A child who is in such an emotional state is unlikely to acquire the needed confidence to cope with life's challenges. As noted earlier, this is a critical component for the development of a healthy self-concept. And it is unrecognized or untreated depression that can be a major detractor in helping the ADHD child to achieve this goal.

In conclusion, the importance of identifying and treating the ADHD child's depression must not be under-rated. As the research shows, the symptoms of depression do not just disappear with the passage of time. Rather, they appear to intensify and carry into the adult years. There is an old saying, "An ounce of prevention is worth a pound of cure." This surely needs to be considered in treating children who are afflicted with depression as well as ADHD.

NOTES

1. Jeffrey Bernstein, "When ADHD Combines with Depression," *Depression can Often Co-exist with AD/HD 2003*, http://www.drjeffonline.com/ow/?d=1643152.0374 (26, January 2006).

2. David Robiner, "ADHD and Depression," Focus *Adolescent Services 2000*, http://www.focus.com/ADHD-Depression.html (26, January 2006).

3. Anxiety and Depression Solutions, "Common Disorders Associated with ADHD" 2004, http:www.anxiety-and-depresion-solutions.com/articles/adhddisorder010305 .htm (26 January 2006).

4. Peter Jensen, "Attention-Deficit/Hyperactivity Disorder," About Mental *Illness 2003*, http://www.nami.org/Templatecf.../TagedPageDisplay.cfm8TPLID=54ContentID =2304 (26, January 2006).

5. Erik Erikson, *Childhood and Society* (New York: Norton, 1963).

6. Robert J. Havighurst, *Developmental Tasks and Education* (New York: D. McKay, 1979).

7. American Psychiatric Association, *Quick Reference to the Diagnostic Criteria from DSM-IV* (Washington, DC: American Psychiatric Association, 1994), 168–172.

8. Public Service Ad by Google, "Childhood Depression" *Fighting Depression 2006*, http://www.fightingdepression.co.uk/Fighting-depression/xhildhood_depression.asp. (26, January 2006).

Chapter Three

Depression: The Underlying Cooperation "Killer"

As the preceding indicates, the ADHD child experiences a myriad of negative emotions at varying levels of intensity. Chronic anxiety and sadness can quickly escalate into an intense fear of being overwhelmed, accompanied by feelings of despondency and hopelessness. It is during these times that the ADHD child's behavior may become even more erratic and uncontrollable. Emotionally distraught ADHD children have much more difficulty concentrating and completing assigned tasks. Moreover, they may act-out repeatedly, engaging in one impulsive behavior after another. Corrections, punishments, the promise of rewards for good behavior, and even encouragement often fail to curb their seemingly self-destructive course. Their inability to regain and sustain self-control occurs because they are in a state of "emotional overload." Like an out of control automobile, the ADHD child is simply unable to regulate his or her emotional accelerator so that an inevitable "crash course" can be avoided. And more importantly, the child is not motivated to do so. Rather, he or she appears to care less about the outcomes of his or her actions.

How often do we hear a frustrated ADHD child say, "I don't care," when the consequences of their errant actions are pointed out to them. The truth is that rampaging ADHD children, who are in the midst of an impulsively driven temper out-burst, do not care. The temporary gain of venting their frustration and the attention that they receive (even though it is negative) are worth whatever the consequences might be. And at least for this moment in time, he or she is a formidable force who parents, teachers, and peers cannot ignore. And commanding such attention, despite the negativity attached to it, is preferable to being ignored or disregarded. This is especially true if the child believes that even his or her most valiant efforts to perform successfully would be useless anyway. For some young people infamy trumps fame, particularly when they view the latter as being unattainable. If the child is good at being, "bad," why waste effort trying to achieve the former, especially if the youngster perceives this as an exercise in futility. More on this topic will be presented in Chapter 14, which focuses upon the importance of self-confidence.

When a child believes that he or she is incapable of performing successfully, it is most likely that hopelessness will become the dominant emotional force influencing his or her actions. Such a despondent state can be easily overlooked, however. When we see a child act recklessly, fail to follow the rules, and treat others in a recalcitrant and cavalier fashion, such behavior can easily arouse negative feelings within us. This is particularly true when we view such activity as being willfully belligerent. This can cause us to want to get "a pound of flesh" from what we perceive to be a spiteful, mean spirited child.

It is important to recognize, however, that the ADHD child's frustration, anger, and acting-out behavior are the symptoms, not the genesis of his or her problem. At the root of the child's difficulties is an oftentimes unrecognized despondency and hopelessness. This is easy to overlook because we typically think of despondency, which could develop into a serious form of depression, in a different light than the behavior that is ordinarily exhibited by ADHD children. Despondency or depression is usually associated with withdrawal, sadness, emotional malaise, tearfulness, a somber appearance, and a generalized apathy affecting all aspects of the child's life. Viewing a youngster in this state usually evokes feelings of sympathy, concern, and protectiveness within us. These emotions are in marked contrast to those that we experience when we are required to deal with an acting-out ADHD child. However, it is imperative that we recognize that impulsivity, belligerency, a lack of concentration, and a failure to follow rules can become exacerbated if the child's affective state is a hopeless one. Again, if the child perceives him or herself in a negative light, believing that he or she is incapable of performing successfully, then acting-out, poor concentration, and belligerency will follow.[1] While these may not be the expected signs associated with childhood depression, nevertheless, it is depression, hopelessness, and even outright despair that can be the fuel driving the ADHD youngster's annoying, counterproductive, and antisocial actions. And it is these underlying emotions, which must be addressed and altered if the child is to be helped.

No matter how well an educational or therapeutic plan is conceived, it is the child's attitude and emotional disposition that will ultimately determine whether he or she cooperates and enthusiastically participates in the program. Even the most carefully designed and implemented approaches by parents, educators, and mental health professionals can be sabotaged by a persistently stubborn and uncooperative child. It is imperative, therefore, that the ADHD youngster's current cognitive and emotional disposition be given prime consideration in the formation of any treatment approach that is to be put into practice at home and school. Again, to overlook or to give only cursory attention to these significant psychodynamic factors could undermine even the most skillfully crafted behavior modification and educational programs.

NOTE

1. American Psychiatric Association, *Quick Reference To The Diagnostic Criteria From DSM-IV* (Washington DC: American Psychiatric Association, 1994), 161–171.

Chapter Four

The Acquisition of Empathy: The First Step in Helping Depressed ADHD Children

Empathy is a psychological term that is battered around by educators, mental health professionals, and lay people alike. Some people confuse empathy with sympathy, pity, or the unconditional love of another person. However, empathy is none of the above. Rather, it is the ability to actually walk in someone else's shoes. Empathy requires that we experience the internal world of another person by actually trying to put ourselves in his or her place. When we empathize with another human being, we can feel what that person feels; think what he thinks; and understand why he acted as he did.[1,2,3] Empathy does not mean that we approve of someone else's behavior or that we feel sorry for him. It merely requires that we are able to perceive the world in the same manner as the person with whom we are interacting.

While many people might believe that it is easy to empathize with others, this is farthest from the truth. In order to empathize, we have to be objective. This means that we must temporarily put aside our own feelings in order to understand those emotional, intellectual, and social factors that are motivating or driving the other person's behavioral engine. Setting aside our own feelings or disengaging from a "power struggle" in which an unreasonable youngster appears to be intentionally trying to "pluck our nerves" can be a daunting task. After all, because we are adults, we believe that we are deserving of respect. Moreover, we are usually objectively correct when we criticize the child's errant behavior and insist that he or she make an immediate effort to correct it.

Unfortunately, logic and right reasoning have little impact on the ADHD child who is caught in the locking grip of an emotional quagmire. It is not objectivity but the child's subjective impressions that are the propelling force behind every self-defeating action that we observe. Unless we understand this

11

and can make a plan to correct it, there is little chance that the behavioral improvements that we seek will take place.

How many times have we interacted with an emotionally distraught youngster who is angry about some perceived injustice with a parent, a sibling, a peer, or a teacher that might have occurred several weeks or even months ago? How many times might the child have vented his or her frustration over the fact that this injustice was never recognized by those in authority and still remained uncorrected to this day? The unrelenting teasing of peers, the insensitive criticism of adults, or being blamed for over-reacting to the harassment of classmates are not easily forgotten. The negative affective residue of such incidents continues to be mulled over in the child's mind. These fester like an untreated cold sore that never heals. Even though the pain might be temporarily forgotten during the tranquil times, it still remains deeply embedded in the unconscious recesses of the child's psyche. This becomes most readily apparent when the next power struggle emerges over an issue concerning "fairness." The youngster is quick to air out the dirty laundry from the past as a justification for his or her overactive behavior or rule violation.

One might ask, what does all of this have to do with the importance of empathy? The answer to this question is simple enough. It is empathy that enables us to diffuse the child's excessive emotionality and helps him to put his affective life into proper perspective. The child who perceives an adult as understanding, accepting, and caring is most likely to be receptive to what the adult says to him or her.[4,5] Children are much more likely to argue, to make excuses and to react with hostility when they think that we are against or "out to get" them. Even sincere, well-meaning adults, who actually care deeply for problem children, will fail to influence them unless they are perceived as being empathetic. That is how important empathy just happens to be! It is the primary ingredient upon which all helping relationships are built, especially those with troubled children and adolescents.

As noted earlier, empathy requires that we be objective and that we temporarily suspend our judgment about the "goodness" or "badness" of the child's actions. We must ask ourselves, "How would I feel if I was this child? How would I think if I was diagnosed with ADHD? How would I behave if I felt and thought in the same way as this youngster?" By stepping back and attempting to answer these questions, we can envision what it is like to walk in the child's shoes. Once this is accomplished, we will have achieved the goal of being empathetic. This is the key that unlocks the door to understanding those emotional demons that can fuel the fire of the ADHD child's impulsivity, inattention, and behavioral overreactions.

In order to become empathetic, it is important to construct a profile of those characteristics and situations that impact on the ADHD child. We must then ask ourselves how we would feel if we had to confront these. For instance, we might ask ourselves the following: "How would I feel if:

I acted impulsively and couldn't understand why I behaved this way?

I couldn't complete my work because I was so easily distracted?

I had to take pills because I couldn't control my behavior?

I was constantly teased, ridiculed, and bullied by my peers?

My parents were always frustrated with me because I behaved so poorly?

My teachers always complained to my parents about my poor self-control?

I repeatedly moved from one school program to another because nobody was able to help me?

My parents said that they "had tried everything" but they were just unable to get me to behave responsibly?

I had to see a psychiatrist for pills and a counselor because my parents and teachers thought I was crazy?

I believed that I was stupid and couldn't learn like other kids?

My siblings did well in school, had friends, and were invited places, but I was always left out?

I was too hyper to participate in community activities, and when I tried, the adults would call my parents and complain because I "didn't fit in?"

I was told that I had ADHD at the age of six and that my "special needs" meant that I had to be taught differently than the other kids in my class?

I had to have extra tutoring after school because, unlike other kids, I didn't get it the first time around?

How would I feel if these things happened to me"

The chances are that if I answered these questions honestly, I would feel considerable emotional pain. It would be immensely hurtful to know that I was not measuring up to the expectations of my parents and teachers. Moreover, believing that my classmates considered me to be "stupid" would be particularly painful. The chances are that I would be sad at best and markedly depressed at worst. How can anyone feel good about themselves when they perform so poorly day after day? And worst of all, you would never hear the end of it! That, in and of itself, would be most grating on the nerves.

But besides being hurt, the chances are that I would be angry, even furious. I didn't chose to have ADHD and consciously decide to become academically and socially different. And the fact that few, if any, people understand me would enrage me even further. Adults are supposed to be compassionate and guide children. Yet all that I received were admonitions and a belly full of criticisms. Kindness, encouragement, and patience are in short supply when you are an ADHD kid. These are the kind of statements that I would probably be saying to myself. Like any wounded soul, many ADHD children react accordingly. They are ready to be combative, even before the first words of an interchange are spoken.

As one can plainly see, diffusing this intense pain is of the utmost importance. Without this, academic growth is likely to proceed slowly at best, and the youngster's social growth will stagnate. Diffusion begins by acknowledging the child's emotional pain and giving credence to the feelings and perceptions that spawn them. After all, anyone of us would be frustrated if this affliction were thrust upon us, particularly during our most youthful and promising years. Therefore, when the child is venting his or her frustration, it would be far better to verify what the child feels and to identify why he or she feels this way.

For example, a child might complain that he was unfairly sent out of the classroom for being noisy. He claims that the other children were also engaging in this kind of behavior. In a firm but soothing voice, the caretaker might say, "You're really angry that the teacher put you out of the classroom for making noises. Other kids were doing the same thing but that did not happen to them. You resent being singled out by the teacher. And you are frustrated because you think that this is unfair and that nothing is being done about it. No wonder you are angry. If I was in your shoes, I would feel the same way."

Pause at this point. The pause gives the child the time to integrate what you have said. It provides the child with the opportunity to examine his or her feelings and the perceptions responsible for them. Moreover, your response demonstrates that you empathize with the child's plight. Again, this increases the likelihood that he or she will be more receptive to the corrective information that is to follow.

Notice that in the preceding example the helping adult did not say that the child's perception was accurate or that the youngster should not be penalized for making noises. Rather, the child's feelings and the thoughts attached to them were verified along with an acknowledgment that, "If I viewed things in this way, I too would be frustrated."

As noted earlier, such an empathic response helps to remove the defensiveness that interferes with the child's potential to learn. It creates a more benign and receptive environment that can facilitate both the social and emotional growth within the child. After the pause and the calm that follows, we can insert the pivotal words of "however" or "but," which pave the way for the presentation of new information for the youngster's consideration. The new information will enable the child to reevaluate the problem, to correct his or her errant thinking, and to gain greater self-control. However, what follows the pivotal words is the subject of another chapter.

NOTES

1. Carl R. Rogers, "The Necessary and Sufficient Conditions of Therapeutic Personality Change," *Journal of Consulting Psychology* no. 2(1957): 459–461.

2. Carl R. Rogers, "Characteristics of a Helping Relationship," *American Personnel and Guidance Journal 37*, no.1(1958): 6–16.

3. C. H. Patterson, *Theories of Counseling Psychology* (New York: Harper & Row, 1973), 388.

4. Paul Lavin, *Profiles in Fury* (East Rockaway, Ny: Cummings & Hathaway, 1998), 90–100.

5. Paul Lavin and Cynthia Park, *Despair Turned into Rage* (Washington, DC: CWLA Press, 1999), 55–60.

Chapter Five

The Adult-Child Relationship: The Catalyst for Change

The importance of empathy, which has been emphasized in the previous chapter, is the springboard for forming a trusting, caring relationship with the ADHD child. It is this ongoing relationship with at least one significant adult that is essential to lowering and eliminating the ADHD child's defensive thinking, thereby making him or her emotionally more malleable to change. The literature clearly indicates that the formation of a viable adult-child relationship, particularly with troubled youth, should be of the highest priority.[1,2]

Erik Erikson, a well-known developmental psychologist, postulated that children and adults are confronted with critical psychosocial conflicts as they pass from one stage of development to the next throughout the lifespan.[3] The positive resolution of these has a marked impact on the healthy social and emotional development of each person. The first and most important psychosocial conflict, which occurs during infancy, is trust versus mistrust.

Whether children develop a trusting or mistrusting orientation toward life is largely determined by the quality of the early relationship that they have with the significant adults in their lives, particularly their parents. If adults are loving, caring, and meet the child's needs as they arise, then he or she is much more likely to develop a positive view of other people. Moreover, feelings of being valued, a sense of personal security, and a confident and optimistic orientation toward life itself are fostered.

Mistrusting children, on the other hand, begin to view life quite differently. They expect to be ignored and even rejected. A cynical orientation toward people begins to develop. The youngster is more likely to lack confidence and expect to do poorly. As a result, defensiveness, surliness, withdrawal, and acting-out occur with greater and greater frequency. Unfortunately, children who are mistrusting become locked into an emotional straight jacket that deters them from moving forward.

There is another important reason why establishing a trusting relationship is so necessary. Children who trust adults are usually free of those psychological "hang-ups" that can interfere with their cognitive, social, and emotional growth. They believe that adults care about them and that they are committed to looking out for their best interests. Because their orientation is positive, these young people respond favorably to parents, teachers, and community members. As a result, they are much more receptive toward learning the lessons of life that are being taught to them.

Mistrusting children hardly ever respond in this fashion. Rather, they constantly question and rebel against authority. Asking "why," claming that they "don't care," and challenging the amount and quality of those tasks assigned to them occur constantly. Because they are emotionally encumbered by their mistrust, they literally refuse to learn from those adults who are sincere and could be of the utmost benefit in helping them. Although these young people may be experiencing great emotional pain, they seldom will admit this. Rather, withdrawal, hostility, defiance, and other negative reactions associated with this deep emotional hurt occur with frequency. And this is what we may observe day in and day out in our interactions with them.

The preceding goes back to the original point in this chapter. It is the establishment of a proper relationship with the child that is the foundation upon which real learning is built. In examining this more closely, we might compare the child's mind to a potentially fertile piece of ground. While the potential for growth exists, the plot must be tilled and prepared properly if the seeds, which are planted into the soil, are to germinate and fruitfully mature. The adult-child relationship is the tiller of the child's mind. This is what prepares the ground work for the proper reception and integration of new information, which is conveyed to him or her. If the adult-child relationship is not fostered and nurtured over time, then the opposite is likely to occur. The child will not be receptive to what is presented. No matter how many seeds we plant and sow, they will consistently fail to produce fruit. This is why the importance of the adult-child relationship is so significant. It sets the tone for real and sustained learning in the years to come.

To form a good relationship with a despondent and rebellious ADHD child is a formidable task. It requires time, patience, and persistence. Moreover, it requires that we accept the child as is, with no strings attached. As stressed previously, this does not mean that we approve of everything that the child does. After all, inappropriate behavior needs to be addressed and corrected accordingly. However, it means that even though the child is behaving badly, we are able to continue caring and show that we have his or her best interest

at heart. Maintaining this attitude is far from easy, especially when the youngster is challenging our authority. But continuing to have confidence in the
child, even in the midst of a battle, is critical to ultimately helping him or her
to eventually make progress. Keep in mind that defensive ADHD children are
often poor learners. Their psychological energy is used in making excuses,
venting their frustration, and trying to out-fox us in a game of intellectual hide
and seek. This is why fostering a warm, caring, and accepting relationship is
so critical to their educational progress. It is an antidote for eliminating those
emotional blocks that interfere with the child's learning.

NOTES

1. C.N. Shealy, "From Boys Town to Oliver Twist: Separating Fact from Fiction in
Welfare Reform and Out-of-Home Placement of Children and Youth." *American Psychologist 50*, no.8 (August, 1995): 565–580.

2. Paul Lavin, *Profiles in Fury* (East Rockaway, NY: Cummings and Hathaway,
1998), 94–100.

3. Erik Erikson, *Childhood and Society* (New York: Norton, 1963).

Chapter Six

More on the Adult-Child Relationship: Inspiring the ADHD Child to Please You

A short time ago, I had an eleven year old ADHD student in my office. He had been referred because his conduct, while not totally outrageous, was blatantly inappropriate for his age level. What was most striking, however, were the reasons that he gave on why he should not act in such an immature fashion. Repeatedly I asked him why engaging in such obnoxious behavior was such a bad choice. The answer was that given most frequently was "Because I could get into trouble." Further attempts to get him to think more deeply about the potential consequences of his actions produced the same answer. This young man appeared to be bewildered and even confused that there might be a more profound reason as to why he should avoid behaving foolishly. It barely occurred to him that disappointing his teachers and parents, losing his self-respect and the respect of others, and that setting a bad example for our younger students were good reasons for not acting badly.

Because his moral reasoning was so immature, I tried to lead him into thinking more deeply on how his actions impacted on his parents, teachers, and peers. After awhile, he seemed to grasp the point that I was trying to convey to him. However, it took much effort to grease his intellectual wheels in my attempt to get him to explore this issue from a more advanced social and moral perspective. Treading this road seemed to be a new experience for him. He simply had not reflected on the multiple consequences of his actions and how these affected those around him.

Self-centeredness is not a new phenomenon for children. It is even expected to some degree. However, the "I shouldn't do it because I'll get into trouble" response, was unsatisfactory at this young man's age level. In fact, a person whose moral reasoning fails to advance beyond this point has very little incentive for acting civilly or for following societal rules. It is true that the fear of being punished can deter one from behaving badly. However, if the fear of punishment is non-existent or if the chances are good that a person can get away with violating the rules, then it is far more likely that inappropriate and even antisocial behavior will increase in frequency.

The answer as to why the preceding would occur is simple enough if we apply the principles of behavioral psychology to this scenario. Wrong behavior often produces immediately beneficial results from which the violator can derive great pleasure, temporary power over others, or even a reputation for being "cool." If the chances of getting away with breaking a rule are reasonably good, the conniving mind of a recalcitrant child can easily find some way to do it. And the more times that he or she is successful in avoiding the negative consequences, the more likely it is that the behavior will be repeated. The inadvertent repetitive reinforcement of inappropriate and uncivil behavior only strengthens bad habits. At some point in the future, a high price will have to be paid for the momentary gains that this produces. However, before this occurs, the youthful recalcitrant can arrogantly bask in the glory of defying authority and gaining the notoriety attached to this rebellion. The youngster's "look at me" mantra becomes the solidification of excessive self-centeredness, which is so repugnant to those young people who are cooperative and try to do what's right.

How does this relate to the adult-child relationship one might ask at this point. As noted in previous chapters, the establishment of an emotional attachment or "bonding" with at least one significant adult is the most important catalyst in helping the ADHD child to change his or her errant views. Make no mistake about it. Not engaging in deviant behavior simply because one wants to avoid being punished falls at the lowest level of moral reasoning, which is typically characteristic of very young children. It is not typical of latency age youngsters and those who are approaching adolescence, however.[1,2]

In summation, the acting-out ADHD child, whose only concern is being caught and punished, is merely going to look for better opportunities to get away with his or her deviant behavior. A youngster may openly acknowledge that some act is wrong. However, because the act is pleasant and provides immediate gratification, the incentive for engaging in it still remains. Unless the child perceives his or her wrongdoing in a different light, he or she will simply connive and scheme until the odds for getting away with errant behavior are in his or her favor.

As stressed throughout this book, depressed and frustrated ADHD children often perceive themselves as being unloved by the adults in their lives. They are, therefore, likely to be mistrusting, hostile, and self-centered. Because their need for affection has never been met, strong feelings of hurt and even rage can propel them into engaging in impulsive, self-gratifying acts that pay no heed to the rules of society and those who promote them. Moreover, the repetition of this egocentric, careless, and sometimes senseless acting-out only reinforces more self-centeredness and the negative, defensive thinking associated with this. Again, "bonding" or the emotional attachment to significant adults is critical in helping young people to become stable, socially integrated and productive citizens.[3] It is this attachment that enables children to develop a caring attitude, an attitude in which feelings of remorse and disappointment in themselves for letting down those adults who love them is founded. When young people care about what adults think and want to please them, they are far more likely to be open minded and receptive to that which is presented to them. This wisdom, which is conveyed to them by caring adults, can then set the tone for bringing about a more advanced level of moral reasoning and the willingness to do what is right for the betterment of all members of society.

The ADHD child, who is motivated to please adults and engages in kind acts in the service of others, becomes a credit to his or her family, school, and community. However, before the child can achieve this goal, his or her psyche must be prepared to receive and integrate the "right thinking" that is taught to him or her. As noted previously, it is our positive, caring, and loving relationship that tills the child's mind and prepares it for the seeds of wisdom, which are planted there. And it is the continuation of this relationship that enables the seeds to germinate and to produce the sound philosophical foundation upon which the highest levels of ethical and socially appropriate behavior are based. In order to achieve this objective, however, the ADHD child must be inspired to please the adults in his or her life and not be impulsively driven to work in opposition to them.

NOTES

1. Lawrence A. Kohlberg, *The Meaning and Measurement of Moral Development* (Worcester, MA: Clark University Press, 1980).

2. Paul Lavin, *Working with Angry and Violent Youth* (Columbia, MO: Hawthorne Educational Services, 1996), 25–26.

3. Paul Lavin and Cynthia Park, *Despair Turned Into Rage* (Washington, DC: CWLA Press, 1999), 57–80.

Chapter Seven

Defensive Thinking: The Importance of Recognizing Destructive Thought Patterns

As emphasized in the previous chapters, empathy enables us to understand the ADHD child's point of view. Moreover, it lays the foundation for establishing a viable child-adult relationship. However, being empathetic goes beyond a mere understanding of how the youngster typically feels. A truly empathetic parent, educator, or mental health professional is able to acquire an in-depth grasp of the ADHD youngster's hidden and unrecognized thought processes as well. Even the child is often unaware of these thoughts and how he or she unintentionally manipulates them in order to lessen the emotional pain of being labeled as an ADHD misfit.

Because ADHD children are immature and are often in the thrall of intense emotional pain, it is quite commonplace for them to react defensively, even when beneficial criticism from well-meaning adults is given to them. Thinking and behaving defensively seem to be an ordinary part of their repertoire. However, it is important to keep in mind that it is the former that spawns the latter. In other words, it is the child's muddled, confused, and errant thoughts that drive his or her behavior engine.[1,2,3] Because the youngster is only partly aware of these at best, he or she has very little, if any, control of them. As a result, mood swings and "off the wall" behavior follow. Thus, it is the ADHD child's errant and defensive mode of thought that must be identified and corrected if progress is to occur. Once the youngster becomes more reality based in his or her thinking, emotional stability, better choice making, and improved coping skills are far more likely to become an integral part of his or her cognitive and behavioral repertoire.

As the preceding stresses, the understanding of errant thinking and the habitual defensive patterns of thoughts flowing from this are of the utmost importance in altering the ADHD child's feeling and actions. An examination of defensive thinking and how this negatively impacts upon the ADHD young-ster's ability to solve problems is, therefore, a necessary precursor, which must first be undertaken in order to set the stage for positive changes to oc-cur.

ADHD children who behave poorly are quick to deny or to distort the facts when they are faced with their mistakes, failures, and bad judgment. When confronted with the harsh reality of their errant ways, they often become im-mediately overly anxious, despondent, and frustrated. Although there is a lit-tle, subconscious voice that tells them that they are in error, they hardly pay any attention to this. Instead, they ignore this internal signal and vociferously insist that what they did was justified and acceptable. It is important to note that the defensive child's demoralization and the escalation of his or her emo-tional intensity, which is attached to this, are not the product of rational plan-ning or clear thinking. Rather, this process occurs automatically. In other words, as noted previously, the child who is reacting defensively is unaware or only partly aware of what is occurring within him or her. Hence, he or she is at the mercy of these unrecognized and uncontrolled psychodynamic forces, which have such a powerful influence on his or her actions.

Because defensive ADHD youngsters are only marginally aware of those emotional and cognitive factors influencing their behavior, they often act like the poorly tuned engine of an automobile. The improper firing of their psy-chic mechanisms leads to much sputtering, lurching, and inconsistency in performance. Eventually the child's defensiveness can cause a breakdown in his or her capacity to function at home, in school, and in the community. Chronically defensive behavior can have devastating repercussions. Strained interpersonal relationships, self-centeredness, and poor school performance plague those who are cursed with this bad habit. Unless ADHD children can become more fully aware of those internal dynamics causing their defensive-ness, it is unlikely that they will be able to correct this problem. Rather, they will continue to be the victims of this habitually negative psychodynamic pat-tern, which can become more deeply engrained with the passage of time.

As just indicated, defensive children can quickly become enslaved by their own emotional negativity. In order to cope with the underlying conflicts that arouse these emotions, they often rely on defense mechanisms, which can be-come a habitual pattern of counterproductive thinking. In short, defensive mechanisms are mental tricks or seemingly plausible excuses that we make up in order to justify our errant actions. While these excuses might make us feel better for the moment, they fail to address the reasons why we failed to perform successfully. Again, these mechanisms "kick in" so to speak without much fore-thought or planning. They are often an automatic response to the negative emo-tions that we happen to be experiencing at that moment. Unfortunately, reliance on these results in a waste of valuable psychic energy. They cause ADHD children to direct this energy inward in an attempt to protect their bruised and battered ego. This unproductive use of this psychic energy leaves the youngster with little strength for the more adaptive functions requiring right reasoning and problem solving.

As noted earlier, defense mechanisms do have some benefits. This is why ADHD children might rely on them. Defense mechanisms temporarily help the youngster feel better for the moment. However, they do not address the real problems that are causing the child to function so poorly. The reliance on defense mechanisms is self-defeating over the long run. If not corrected, they can seriously undermine the quality of the child's life. Some defense mechanisms, which are particularly problematic, are as follows[4]:

1. Denial. Children who engage in denial refuse to acknowledge evident facts. Even when faced with the obvious, they claim that they do not understand or that something isn't so. They are children who deny the obvious and quickly and emphatically say "NO" when confronted with wrongdoing. Their jaded version, which is contrary to the evidence, is not only presented but insisted upon as being right.
2. Repression. Children who rely on repression refuse to think about problems. When a problem surfaces, they make statements such as, "I don't want to talk about it." They attempt to keep from awareness that which is troubling them. "I don't know," and "I don't care," are typical responses of children who rely on repression.
3. Displacement. Displacement might be used by children who experience strong feelings of anger or frustration toward someone or something that threatens them. Because they fear that they might be harmed, however, they repress the expression of these feelings. They then discharge their frustration on to someone or something, which is not threatening to them. For example, a boy might be angry with the school bully, but he is fearful of retaliation if he fights back. He, therefore, represses his frustration. Later that day, the boy beats up his younger brother claiming that he "made a face" at him. This is his way of discharging the anger, which is actually directed at the bully.
4. Rationalization. Children who rationalize make plausible or what they believe are socially acceptable excuses to justify their behavior. Even though these rationalizations appear to be acceptable, they are actually used to avoid facing a problem. For example, an obese youngster makes up his mind that he needs to go on a diet. When he awakens hungry the next morning, he eats a ponderous amount of food. He then feels guilty because he did not stick to his plan. In order to make himself feel better, he states,

"Everybody needs a good breakfast to start the day. Beside, I wouldn't be able to concentrate on my school work if I was hungry." While this excuse may take away the child's feeling of guilt, the obesity problem still remains. It should be noted that rationalization is one of the most commonly used defense mechanisms.

5. Reaction Formation. This occurs when children express an emotion, which is actually the opposite of what they really feel. For example, the boy who is angry and fearful of the bully acts very friendly toward him. He may even contend that the bully is "cool" and that he likes him.

6. Projection. Projection is a defense mechanism in which children see their faults in everyone else but themselves. For example, a child who tells lies claims that everyone else fails to tell the truth. Or if the child is caught engaging in some offense, the claim is made that, "Everyone else was doing it too." Projection is a common form of blaming used by ADHD children.

The importance of helping ADHD children to identify defensive thinking should not be under-rated. Recognizing and acknowledging this is a critical step in helping the child to alter his or her emotional and behavioral negativity. As parents, educators, and mental health professionals, it is our responsibility to help our young people to minimize the use of defense mechanisms and to utilize their psychological energy so that they can become successful problem solvers. The development of self-insight is a major step toward achieving this goal.

NOTES

1. Paul Lavin, *Teaching Kids to Think Straight* (Columbia, MO: Hawthorne Educational Services, 1991), 3–7.

2. Paul Lavin and Kathryn Lavin, *A Comprehensive Guide for Parenting the ADHD Child* (Baltimore, MD: Publish America, 2005), 78–91.

3. Paul Lavin, *Punishment Devolution: The "Missing Link" in Rearing Today's Children* (Baltimore, MD: Publish America, 2006), 52–61.

4. Paul Lavin, *Teaching Kids to Think Straight* (Columbia, MO: Hawthorne Educational Services, 1991), 3–7.

Chapter Eight

Perception: Its Critical Importance in Understanding ADHD Children

In the previous chapters, the focus was on defensive mechanisms and how these negatively impact on the ADHD child's thinking, affect and behavior. Although I do not want to belabor this point, an in-depth understanding of the ADHD child's perceptions and why these can be so difficult to alter are critical to his or her successful treatment. For those parents, educators, and mental health professionals, who work with ADHD youth, a cursory knowledge of such will just not do. In light of this, therefore, the next two chapters will delve more deeply into these topics. Again, the significance of acquiring an in-depth understanding of the ADHD child's perception must not be underrated.

As noted previously, the old saying, "One man's meat is another man's poison" was constructed in order to make this point. Simply interpreted, this means that our individual view of things is largely responsible for our behavior. Two people with similar backgrounds can react differently to the same stimulus. Even though their backgrounds may be alike, one person interprets the event in a certain way while the other interprets it in an entirely different light. As a result of their differing view, both parties, even though they may share much in common, act differently. For example, in the political arena, one candidate is revered by his or her supporters. That same candidate, on the other hand, is viewed with revulsion by the opposition even though he or she may happen to have grown up in the same generation. The point is that differing philosophical orientations, whether one is aware of them or not, have much to do with why people react in the way that they do. The terms liberal, conservative, and moderate are words that we use to try and simplify what various individuals stand for and how this influences their actions.

Unfortunately, however, human nature is a little more complicated than the "pigeon hole" approach that we use in our attempt to understand others. This is why, even the most ardent supporters of some particular position, are often caught in contradictions, "politically correct" double talk, and out-right lies. Their motives, whether clearly understood or not, mask over what they really believe and, in turn, play a large part in determining how they behave. Clever deception may become a strategic tactic in order to defend an untenable position, which just doesn't quite fit in with what a particular candidate has said or done previously.

The point is that understanding others requires that we examine a multiplicity of factors that might influence their actions. A single dimensional analysis is often grossly inadequate. For example, looking only at the economic sphere and how this might impact on the life of an ADHD child is hardly sufficient in understanding why he behaves as he does. Wealthy children who are afflicted with ADHD may be materially well-cared for. However, the environment in which they are reared may be as emotionally improvised as that of children who are reared in poverty. Their parents may be cold, distant, and even abusive. Their distorted thinking as adults, therefore, may be colored by the unresolved pain, resentment, and anger associated with their childhood years, and their behavior might not be far different than that of the materially impoverished cohort with whom they are being compared. As an aside, it is interest to note that some of our most horrific serial killers came from such a background.[1] This only attests to the fact that the true understanding of others is not an easy task.

Entering the ADHD child's subjective world, seeing life through his eyes, feeling what he feels, thinking what he thinks, and actually trying to vicariously experience what he has gone through is the beginning of real understanding. The next step is to put words on these experiences, to accurately label, define, and interpret these so that greater insight and control can be attained. Again, this is not an easy task. This is why we often err in understanding others and relating effectively to them. Instead of trying to enter their psychic sphere, we settle for parsimonious explanations of their actions. In other words, we "judge a book by its cover." And as we all know, this hardly enables us to truly grasp its contents.

When it comes to understanding human behavior, "judging a book by its cover" can be a serious mistake. For instance, ADHD children, who behave belligerently, can easily be thought of as being "smart-mouth, spoiled brats" who are trying to "jerk us around"(manipulate us). They can instantly arouse our ire and cause us to react in a harsh and punitive fashion. However, as noted previously, their oppositional behavior might actually stem from feelings of alienation, rejection, and frustration because of family discord and misunderstanding. As emphasized earlier, some young people "mess up" to get even with their parents or teachers for what they perceive as unfair treatment. Hence, even when we punish them, they continue to act-out, driving us to the point of distraction. Why? Because the child's real motive is to get revenge. Unless this is understood, no behavioral change is likely to occur despite our best efforts. In other words, the child has to view us in a different light and an "attitude correction" must take place if substantive alterations in behavior are to happen.

"Judging a book by its cover" can be a markedly short-sighted endeavor in attempting to understand why our young people act in the way that they do. Appearances, as we well know, can be quite deceiving. Moreover, judging by appearances can result in a failure to focus on their good attributes, which can so easily be ignored or overlooked.

Make no mistake about it. Adults, as well as children, can easily become the victims of shallow misperceptions if they are not careful. For instances, persons who have money, good looks, and fame can be a source of envy for all of us. Our lack luster lives can spawn feelings of self-pity and resentments about "the breaks that we never got" or "the role of the dice that just never went our way." Such an attitude is counterproductive in our quest for personality growth and maturity. It can cause us to overly focus on what is seemingly important. However, it misses the heart and soul of that which truly exists within the person but cannot be seen with the naked eye. An excellent example of this is a poem by Edward Arlington Robinson, which is as follows:[2]

> Whenever Richard Cory went down town
> We people on the pavement looked at him
> He was a gentleman from soul to crown
> Clean flavored and imperially slim
> And he was always quietly arrayed
> And he was always human when he talked
> But still he fluttered pulses when he said
> "Good morning" and he glittered as he walked
> And he was rich—Yes, richer than a king
> And admirably schooled in every grace
> In fine, we thought he was everything
> To make us wish that we were in his place
> So on we worked, and waited for the light
> And went without meat and cursed the bread
> And Richard Cory one calm summer night
> Went home and put a bullet through his head.

In our quest for the so called "good life" for ourselves and our children, it is easy to misperceive, overlook, and distort that which we see around us. This is why that the fostering of accurate, realistic perceptions about ourselves, other people, and life are so important. It is these impressions which are the driving force behind much of our behavior.

The acquisition of "right thinking" is a skill that does not come about easily or effortlessly. It requires patience, diligence, and the willingness to listen with an unbiased ear to those around us. This is well worth the effort, however. He who hears what other people fail to hear, sees what other people fail to see, and understands what other people do not understand has the power to shape and mold human perception. As mental health professional, educators, and parents, taking control of this endeavor is of the utmost importance, particularly in working with our ADHD children who are often so quickly misjudged by those around them.

NOTES

1. John Douglas, *Mind Hunter* (New York: Scribner, 1995).

2. Arnold Lazarus and Allen Fay. *I Can If I Want To* (New York: Warner Books, 1977), 48–51.

Chapter Nine

Why Perceptual Change Is So Difficult

The ability to be objective is not an easily acquired attribute. Yet this is essential if one is to become truly adept in solving life's problems. Being objective, means being able to distinguish between fact and fiction. Objective persons can identify and interpret factual information without letting their personal feelings, prejudices, or other idiosyncratic material interfere with their analysis. In other words, objective people do not distort or twist the truth in order to satisfy their own unmet needs or create a false reality that suits their particular fancy. To be objective requires that one look reality right in the eye, unequivocally accept its dictates, and take the proper steps to deal with any challenges that this poses. Being objective sounds simple enough. However, putting this into practice is another matter.

All of us have been influenced by events of the past. In some cases, these experiences have had such a powerful impact upon us that they can markedly interfere with our capacity to think clearly. An unrecognized or unacknowledged negatively charged past, which we have failed to address, can prevent us from thinking rationally, particularly when a current challenge, disappointment, or even a minor aversion arises.[1,2]

When I was instructing graduate students, who aspired to become practicing psychotherapists, I used to lecture about "clogged minds" and how emotional "gunk" could interfere with our objectivity. Believe it or not, the inspiration for this lecture was an oil filter commercial that happened to appear on television at that time. In the ad, an actor dressed as a mechanic exhorted the viewers to change the oil filter in their automobiles, replacing it with the brand that he recommended. In the background, a broken down automobile with a sludge clogged oil filter, which was held up for view by the mechanic, were featured. Of course, it was implied that the inattention to the oil filter was responsible for the breakdown of the automobile. The dirty thickened sludge surrounding the filter impeded its ability to cleanse the oil and prevented it from properly lubricating the engine. As a result, the automobile's motor had "burned out" and the car was no longer functional. The mechanic concluded the commercial by stating, "Pay me now or pay me later." The implied message was that it is far better to replace your oil filter now, with their brand of course at a relatively minor expense, than to be negligent and pay a much higher price for major repairs later on.

In my lecture, I compared the poorly functioning human psyche to a sludge clogged oil filter. I emphasized that unconscious needs, deeply engrained prejudices, misdirected passions, and destructive psychological defense mechanisms were the unrecognized "gunk" that prevented the human mind from identifying and processing those facts, which are critical in solving life's problems. Moreover, the free flowing of information was compared to clean oil that lubricates our intellectual pistons so that they can function at full capacity. When emotional "gunk" blocks this free flow, we become cognitively impeded and even impaired in our ability to function successfully.

Again, the sad part of this equation is that even the most well-intentioned people may fail to recognize that this has happened to them. Rather, they may firmly believe that they are thinking and acting rationally, despite the fact that objective evidence would indicate otherwise. All of us have our own subjective emotional baggage from the past. And each of us can be unduly influenced by this if we are not careful. Learning to be objective can be a tough nut to crack, particularly when we have strongly held views and an intense emotional attachment to them. But crack it we must, especially if we are to become adept in understanding the thinking and affect that so profoundly influence the ADHD child's behavior.

The quest for objectivity can be a hard task to master. It requires the ability to keep an open mind and to remain dispassionate while we sift through and attempt to identify the various motives that might be driving the ADHD child's behavioral engine. As emphasized in previous chapters, this can be particularly difficult when it seems that the youngster is deliberately trying to unnerve us, despite our sincere efforts to be helpful. Once caught in this turmoil, it is most tempting to look for simple answers, even though a more patient, in-depth analysis is actually required. The desire to be right, even in the face of contradictory evidence; the desire to please or to be respected by other professionals, educators, and parents who see the child in a negative light; and the propensity to focus only on that which confirms our prejudices must be held in check. The temptation to interpret events so that they support what we want to believe can be tricky business. And what makes this so difficult is that we may not be aware of the fact that we are actually doing this.

Over time, children and adults develop and foster perceptions about themselves, other people, and life itself. These perceptions can be positive or negative, depending on how life's experiences have been interpreted by them. And make no mistake about it. People develop strong emotional attachments to these perceptions. This, in essence, is what makes perception so difficult to change. Perceptions, especially misperceptions, can provide emotional sustenance or solace. It is no wonder that people are so reluctant to change them.

For the ADHD emotionally scared child, giving up misperceptions can be particularly threatening unless we can offer a more viable alternative. The good news, however, is that this can be accomplished, provided that we put into practice those skills, which have been described in previous chapters. As stressed repeatedly throughout this book, empathy and the building of trust are the first steps which must be taken if we are to be successful in this endeavor.

NOTES

1. Arnold Lazarus and Allen Fay, *I Can If I Want To* (New York: Warner Brothers, 1977), 12–14.

2. Albert Ellis, "Emotional Disturbance and its Treatment in a Nutshell," *Canadian Counselor 5, no3.* (1974): 168–171.

Chapter Ten

Restructuring Errant Thinking: The Second Step in Helping ADHD Children

As emphasized previously, empathy is the building block for establishing rapport with the ADHD child. Empathy is the catalyst enabling us to help the child to put words on his or her feelings and perceptions. Moreover, it demonstrates that we understand the ADHD youngster's plight and that we sincerely care about helping him or her. After all, even adults tend to search out persons who understand and accept them when they are confronted with a problem. We want someone whom we trust to be responsible for helping us "to work through our feelings." Children and adolescents are no different. They too want to be understood and to talk with persons who they believe genuinely care about them.

None of us like to be looked down upon, treated with disdain, or ignored. We usually try to avoid those individuals who treat us in this fashion. In fact, such people arouse the worst feelings within us. This makes it very difficult to control ourselves in their presence. If maintaining emotional control is hard for adults in these circumstances, imagine how much more difficult this would be for a child or adolescent. Because of their youth and lack of living experience, they have yet to acquire the maturity and skills for keeping "cool" in the presence of adversity. It's no wonder that ADHD youngsters become frustrated so easily. Again, this is why empathy is so important. It helps to calm the child and to make him or her more receptive to what we have to say.

In chapter 4 on the importance of empathy, I referred to "However" and "But" as pivotal words. These came after the "Pause," which provided some time for the child to cognitively process and integrate the empathetic statements preceding them. An example of how a pivotal word might be inserted after the pause is as follows: "As I said to you, I clearly understand why you have become so frustrated. However, ..." It is at this point that new information can be presented for the child's consideration. It is this new information that identifies the youngster's errant perceptions; how these lead to the intensification and triggering of negative emotions; and how mistaken thinking and negative affect, in combination, lead to impulsive, over-reactive behavior.

In beginning this corrective process, the first step is to point out the erroneous thoughts that are contributing to the child's emotional over-reactions. The trick is to be able to formulate such thoughts into specific words and sentences. The next step involves presenting these to the child and showing him how his "self-talk" is responsible for the intensification of his negative affect. For example, if the child has developed the habit of saying to himself, "I have ADHD. This means that I am dumb and I can't learn," then he is bound to engage in self-pity, which only leads to added frustration, anger, and depression. This thought, of which the child may or may not be consciously aware, must be pointed out to him along with the negative affect that has become attached to it. The helping adult might state, "Because you have ADHD, you believe that you are dumb and stupid and can't learn like other children. No wonder you are frustrated and feel down in the dumps much of the time." After stating this, the helping adult might ask, "What do you think about what I have said? Do you understand that what you think about yourself influences how you feel?" If the child is confused, further explanation can be given until the connection between errant thought and negative emotion is made.

Once the preceding has been accomplished, the second step would be to present a more accurate perception that might be incorporated into the child's thinking. For example, the adult might add, "However, although you have ADHD, this doesn't mean you are dumb and can't learn. In fact, ADHD children are just as smart as their classmates. Having ADHD really means that you actually have more energy than most people. More energy can be a good thing. If your energy is used properly, you might be able to accomplish more than other children. You have the "brain power" to be successful. Your problem is learning how to properly direct and control your energy so that you can achieve this goal." This explanation can be the catalyst for helping the child to replace the errant thought with a more accurate and realistic perception of the problem. After this is presented, again, asking the child what he thinks about your explanation will verify whether he has grasped this concept. If further explanation is needed, it can be provided at this point.

Once the new information is integrated into the child's thinking, his or her emotional state will be altered. Instead of feeling angry and depressed, a sense of hopefulness should arise. Becoming more optimistic would serve as a catalyst for exploring strategies on how the ADHD youngster's energy might be better directed and controlled. Moreover, this approach is more likely to foster a solid rapport between the helping adult and the child, enabling him or her to have a much greater impact in improving the quality of that youngster's life.

Of course, one of the skills needed in effectively implementing the preceding is to be able to recognize and to put into words those errant thoughts that are particularly problematic for ADHD children. Also, being able to formulate more productive thoughts to replace these is needed. Becoming skilled in both of these dimensions is essential in order for this approach to work successfully.

As just emphasized, in order to help ADHD children to replace errant thinking with sensible thinking, we must be able to recognize and to clearly identify the former. Once the child's errant perceptions are specified, the next step would be the formation of productive, realistic thoughts that can be offered as replacements for these. One of the main purposes of this chapter is to identify some of the mistaken notions that this author has found to be particularly problematic for ADHD children.[1] These counterproductive thoughts(CP), along with the productive thoughts (P) that might be used to replace them are as follows:

1. (CP)   I have ADHD. This means that I am stupid and can't learn like other children.

1. (P)   You believe that having ADHD means that you are stupid and can't learn. No wonder you become so frustrated with yourself. However, the truth is that ADHD children can learn and are just as smart as their classmates. ADHD children have problems concentrating. This is why they have difficulty with their school work. This can be improved upon if you are willing to work at it.

2. (CP)   Having ADHD is unfair. It's not my fault that I have this problem. I didn't choose to be this way. Peers and adults should understand this and not criticize me.

2. (P)   You are correct that you did not choose to have ADHD. You're angry because you believe that this has been unfairly thrust upon you. However, think about this. All of us have problems that are not of our choosing. Louis has problems with throwing and catching a ball. Sometimes other kids make fun of this. He can't help having this trouble. Because life is unfair, it makes sense that we should focus on the good things we have and not those things that we can do nothing about. Your ADHD means that you have more energy than most people. Having more energy is a good thing. If you learn to properly manage this energy, then it's possible that you could achieve more than many other children. Keep in mind that everyone who criticizes

you is not trying "to put you down" or hurt your feelings. Many people are just trying to give you good advice on how to do better. If you listen to them and try to follow their suggestions, you will be more likely to succeed.

3. (CP) I have a "chemical imbalance." This prevents me from controlling myself without using pills. Without pills, I can't control my behavior.

3. (P) Because you have ADHD, you believe that you need pills to control your behavior. You feel incapable of controlling yourself without them. It's true that pills can help you to be calm and to concentrate. However, using your brain to think correctly is the most important thing in gaining control of yourself. When you make good choices and behave appropriately, you will be proud of yourself. It is far better for you to be in control of your life, without totally relying on pills. This is what will make you happier and more confident in your ability to be successful.

4. (CP) When something is difficult for me, I shouldn't have to do it. After all, I have ADHD, I can't help getting frustrated when tasks are hard for me.

4. (P) You believe that having ADHD makes it almost impossible to complete difficult tasks. This is why you become so frustrated. However, because you have ADHD doesn't mean that you can't control yourself and complete challenging assignments. If you tell yourself to be calm, and focus on how proud you will be by overcoming your frustration, then you will have a much better chance of acquiring good self-control. This is what will give you the strength to try other challenges in the future. Its up to you to decide whether you want to be confident or not. If you try, the chances are good that you can do it.

5. (CP) Because I have ADHD, other kids tease and make fun of me. People in authority should always stop the teasing and punish those who are responsible for hurting my feelings. Adults should always protect me.

5. (P) When other kids tease you, it hurts your feelings and makes you angry. You believe that adults in authority should stop this from happening and punish the offenders. However, think about this. Some kids will tease and make fun of you because they know it hurts your feelings. They will want you to lose your temper and get into trouble. It is impossible for adults to always catch them when they tease you. You need a better plan for controlling yourself when this happens. Keep in mind that these children want to have fun at your expense. They want to laugh at you and see you get into trouble. You must be determined not to let this happen. If you ignore them and

don't react, they will stop their little game of trying to annoy you. However, you will have to follow this plan for a long time. Remember, you have a certain reputation with them. They expect that you will over-react so they might keep trying to aggravate you for some time. It won't be easy to change them. But with effort, you could succeed. Imagine how good you will feel when you beat them at their own game because you controlled yourself.

6. (CP) Parents owe me. They should give me what I want when I want it. If they don't do as I please, they are being mean.

6. (P) You believe that your parents should always give you what you want and that they are mean when they fail to do so. It's no wonder that you are so frustrated and angry with them. You are right that parents owe you. But let's examine this more carefully. Parents do owe you nutritious food, medical attention, proper clothing, and a public school education. However, they do not owe you luxuries like brand name tennis shoes, junk food, or video games. If they give you these things for free and you behave poorly, your parents will feel resentful because you are not treating them respectfully. You show that you love and respect your parents by the way you treat them. Parents are supposed to guide and teach their children to cope with life's problem. They are here to help you to do what is right, not easy. If your parents don't give you something that you want, it may be that they believe that it is not good for you. This has nothing to do with being mean. Their responsibility is to help you grow up to be a responsible adult. Just giving you what you want would not be the right way for them to treat you.

7. (CP) Life should be the way I want it to be. If things go against me, it is best to get my frustration "out of my system" by venting it at someone or something.

7. (P) You think that taking your frustration out on people or objects around you is the best way to reduce your stress when life goes against you. This explains why you lose your temper so easily. However, let's look at another alternative to reducing your frustration. When you become frustrated, it would be far better to talk to an adult about this rather than taking it out on someone or something. Venting your anger can be destructive to property, or could injure or violate the rights of other people. The consequence for this could be very severe. You could get into trouble with the school, other parents and adults, and even the law. Talking about your problems with an adult who cares about you can better help you to cope with your frustrations much more effectively.

The reader will note that the preceding contains specific words and sentences that can be stated to the child during the restructuring process. It is these "language mediators" that serve as the conduit between the stimulus (an internal or external event) and the emotional arousal (anxiety, anger, depression, etc.) that follow. If these language mediators are inaccurate, incomplete, or distorted then the emotional intensity that the child experiences will be either insufficient to arouse him to engage in some action (an example would be depression, which leads to withdrawal or giving up), or it will become so intense that he will over-react to the situation (an example would be anger, which leads to acting out or explosive behavior). Keep in mind that properly constructed language mediators, which are communicated to the child and integrated into his thinking, will help him to stay on an emotionally stable course. This, in turn, is more likely to bring about a better social adjustment and an improved academic performance.

One final point is worthy of note. The seven CP and P thoughts that were presented are only a few of the self-destructive messages that interfere with the ADHD child's ability to function successfully. There are many other erroneous perceptions, many of which are common to all young people, which may need to be corrected as well. These can be gleaned from other sources written by this author.[2,3,4,5]

NOTES

1. Paul Lavin, "Cognitive Restructuring: A Counseling Approach for Improving the ADHD Child's Self Concept," *Dimensions of Counseling 30, no. 2* (August 2002): 22–27.

2. Paul Lavin and Kathryn Lavin, *A Comprehensive Guide for Parenting the ADHD Child* (Baltimore, MD: Publish American, 2005), 73–85.

3. Paul Lavin and Kathryn Lavin, *Koping for Kids: A Coping Skills Program for Elementary School Children* (Minneapolis, MN: Educational Media Corp, 2005), 11–30.

4. Paul Lavin, *Punishment Devolution: The "Missing Link" in Rearing Today's Children* (Baltimore, MD: Publish America, 2006), 52–61.

5. Paul Lavin, *Teaching Kids to Think Straight* (Columbus, MO: Hawthorne Educational Services, 1991), 3–7.

Chapter Eleven

The ADHD Child's Self-Concept: It's Important in Coping with Environmental Stressors

As indicated previously, many ADHD children have emotional problems that are secondary to or are associated with their disorder. And it is this negative emotionality that interferes with their ability to learn and to function successfully.

Being an ADHD child is not easy. His or her inattention, failure to complete assignments, and impulsivity often result in a steady stream of negative feedback from parents, teachers, and peers. As noted previously, many ADHD children, despite being of at least average intelligence, believe that they are "stupid" and disliked by those around them. The ADHD child, therefore, becomes easily frustrated and quickly over-reacts to even helpful criticism. ADHD children instinctively know that they are different. The stinging reminders of their inadequacies, even from well-meaning people, only rubs salt into the wound. And like any wounded person, they quickly strike back. Arguing, oppositional behavior, and making commends such as "I don't care" or "Whatever" are defensive maneuvers that are unconsciously utilized for the purpose of protecting the little bit of self-esteem that still remains in their bruised and battered ego.

It is no wonder that many ADHD youngsters lack confidence in themselves and mistrust those around them. They often expect to fail, to be chastised, and criticized. This mental set can only leave them in a despondent, overly anxious, and resentful condition. And it is this condition that interferes with the child's ability to learn and to establish viable social relationships. In fact, this negative emotional state can actually produce and exacerbate those symptoms that are characteristic of ADHD. Thus, the failure to listen or stay on task and to behave impulsively may actually worsen. This only makes him or her to appear even more willful and stubborn than usual. Such behavior then elicits more negative reactions from teachers, parents, and peers, which keeps this never-ending counterproductive cycle going.

How do we stop this emotional merry-go-round? We must first recognize that the child's oppositional behavior is the symptom, not the cause of the problem. It is a poor self-concept, the pain of feeling inadequate, that causes the child to react so negatively to those around him.[1,2] It is important, therefore, that we respond in a different fashion than that which the child would expect. As noted earlier, ADHD children often expect others to be critical and to make derogatory comments to them. Hence, instead of chastising the child, we need to emphasize with his plight, conveying in specific language that we fully understand his frustration and why he is feeling this way. This then needs to be followed by encouraging comments, indicating that we have confidence in the child's ability to perform successfully.

It is important to maintain a positive tone of voice in communicating with an often beleaguered ADHD child. If we allow our feelings to get hurt or if we become enraged by his or her sarcastic comments, we will be simply reinforcing the child's faulty notion that "everybody is against me." Responding in the opposite fashion and "keeping your cool" is more likely to produce beneficial results. The child will eventually become more trusting toward you and view you as an advocate, not one of the "enemy." As stressed previously, the youngster's defensiveness will gradually diminish, and he or she will become more receptive to what you have to say. Cooperativeness and improved behavior are then more likely to follow.

There is another point that needs to be reemphasized in understanding the plight of emotionally encumbered ADHD children. Although many youngsters might be diagnosed with ADHD, it is quite possible that anxiety and depression stemming from environmental disruptions are largely responsible for many of the symptoms associated with this disorder. The importance of identifying, modifying, and helping the child to cope with his or her surroundings is of the utmost significance. Again, ADHD children are particularly sensitive to the people and events around them. As noted previously, they are quick to over-react, believing that adults and peers dislike or are unfairly "out to get them." They are, therefore, hypersensitive to a slight smirk, a quick glance in their direction, or two or more persons who might be whispering within an eye-shot from them.

Because many ADHD children truly believe they "are not okay," it is quite common for them to blurt out accusations, have a tantrum, or to whine continuously when such events occur. Significant frustration with themselves and their personal inability to cope are at the root of this problem. Deep down inside, they perceive themselves as being inept and a curse to their parents, teachers, and other adults who interact with them on a daily basis. But it is not the underlying theme of hopelessness that we overtly observe. The child does not recognize this, nor can he or she put this into words. Rather, obnoxious, oppositional, and spiteful behavior become the substitutes for a more introspective and reasoned solution for fixing the problem.

Parents, educators, and mental health professionals need to be attentive to those environmental stressors to which the ADHD child is exposed on a daily basis. It may be that the child's continued, ongoing exposure to these is responsible for his or her failure to concentrate, complete assignments, and to behave appropriately. It should be noted that marital or family discord may be particularly problematic for the ADHD child. Because ADHD children are so difficult to manage, they can place a great deal of stress on parents, siblings, and even extended family members. The problems of coping with them can not only strain the parent's marriage, but the acrimonious environment that this creates can lead to separation and divorce. In this author's experience, this scenario is not uncommon in families with ADHD children. Young children and even adolescents often experience considerable affective turmoil if their parents have a strained relationship or are in the process of separation and divorce. For a child, the shattering of a once intact family, no matter how dysfunctional, is a heart wrenching and painful experience. While the youngster may not talk about the emotional pain associated with this, it does not mean that he or she is unaffected by what is occurring. Rather, it is the opposite of this that is actually taking place.

Numerous and troubling questions can run through the ADHD child's mind. Am I responsible for my parent's breakup? What could I have done to help them to stay together? Will my parents still love me now that they are apart? What should I do when mom talks about dad or when dad talks about mom? Why can't my parents work this out and get back together again? Who really is at fault? Should I take sides or remain neutral? Why do things have to be this way? These are just a few of the questions that can plague a troubled child. Even when they are addressed, uncertainty, insecurity, and confusion associated with the breakup still remain. The hurt, anxiety, depression, and frustration just don't go away that easily. Emotional turmoil and the pain accompanying it repeatedly resurrect themselves.

It is important to recognize that preoccupation with family problems can become overwhelming. Carrying such an emotional burden can absorb so much psychological energy that there is little left over for learning. And how does the child behave in the face of this? He or she fails to attend; important tasks go unfinished; and excuse making, complaining, and whining become rampant. Emotionally encumbered children become easily frustrated. Sometimes they become teary eyed and cry for no apparent reason. At other times they quickly become hostile and defiant, particularly when demands are placed upon them. While emotionally wrought children may exhibit ADHD symptoms, their errant behaviors can be driven by affective rather than bio-chemical forces. It is imperative, therefore, that these unresolved emotional issues be addressed.

We must keep in mind that children are not miniature adults whose behavior is necessarily governed by logic and "right reasoning." Rather, they are emotionally fragile and can become easily undone by adverse environmental conditions. These, in essence, could actually be responsible for the child's ADHD like symptoms and the oppositional behavior associated with them. Simply diagnosing the child with ADHD and providing medication and a behavior management program is unlikely to resolve the problem. In fact, such an over-sight could lead to continued educational and social difficulties. Addressing the child's emotional concerns, therefore, can be of the utmost importance in helping the youngster to make real and sustaining progress. As parents, educators, and mental health professionals, we cannot afford to overlook them.

NOTES

1. Guy R. Francois, *The Lifespan* (Belmont, CA: Wadsworth Publishing Co., 1999), 282–285.

2. Paul Lavin, "Cognitive restructuring: A Counseling Approach for Improving the ADHD Child's Self Concept, "*Dimensions of Counseling 30, no.2* (August, 2002): 22–27.

Chapter Twelve

An ADHD Child Can
Strain a Marriage

Because the ADHD child's parents play such an important role in his or her life, this chapter will follow-up on parental discord and the influence that this has on the youngster's emotional state. Again, parental discord, separation, and divorce are not uncommon in families with ADHD children. And it is the unresolved issues associated with this that can be largely responsible for the child's poor behavior.

ADHD children, whose parents are separated or divorced, may experience a myriad of negative emotions.[1] Young children, particularly those under ten years of age, often assume some responsibility for the parental breakup. As a result, marked feelings of shame and guilt are common. Moreover, if the youngster's behavior led to parental arguments, these feelings would naturally be intensified. Obviously, this could cause the child to experience a chronic state of immense sadness, which if not unearthed and openly addressed, would only worsen. Again, such emotional strain may exacerbate the child's ADHD symptoms, leading to withdrawal or acting-out behavior. In light of the preceding, it makes good sense for parents to put their personal issues aside in order to better address the needs of their children. Working together, despite their differences, and putting the youngster first is the most logical course of action. Communicating with each other in a civil fashion and improving their parental skills can be of significant benefit in helping their child to work through his or her emotional turmoil so it does not interfere with his or her ability to function at home and school.

While the preceding may be considered to be good advice, its implementation, if this occurs at all, often comes after the fact. It is quite conceivable that had these recommendations been in place during the marriage, the divorce might have never occurred in the first place. After all, it is not the child who causes the divorce. It is the failure of the parent's relationship. Perhaps their inability to communicate with each other from the beginning is at the root of the problem.

There is no question that poor communication and the deficiencies in the relationship itself can ruin a marriage. However, just having an ADHD child can produce parental controversies, "tweak" one's nerves, and magnify the most glaring of out human weaknesses. Many of the ordinary problems that can strain a marriage become exacerbated when one is also required to parent an ADHD youngster. Rearing children who are not afflicted with ADHD, learning disabilities, and secondary emotional problems is difficult enough given today's hectic societal climate. Adding these negative dimensions into the child's personality mix can create a "parenting circus," if one is not adequate prepared for this challenge.

When people enter into the matrimonial state, they usually begin their life together with optimism, love, and a firm dedication and commitment to each other. Why would anyone enter into a marriage anticipating interpersonal acrimony and that a contentious and hostile divorce were on the horizon? More often than not, we are at our best when we begin this hopeful venture. During courtship, couples are usually "on the same page" so to speak. They would hardly anticipate that the birth of an ADHD child could potentially severely undermine the strong bond that exists between them.

As just indicated, this may all change when the newly arrived ADHD child enters the scene. Now Mom may have to stay up half the night trying to sooth their colicky, disgruntled infant. She becomes tired and frustrated because the emotional reciprocity that is supposed to exist between mother and child is non-existent. Her prized possession is constantly squirming when she tries to hold him, and he seems to be repelled by, instead of responding to her gentle touch. Dad, on the other hand, also becomes frustrated. There never seems to be any peace in the house. Coming home after working all day is like going to a second job. The "A man's home is his castle" platitude becomes a myth that is quickly shattered.

As the years pass, life hardly gets any better. ADHD Junior is constantly on the go. Mom feels like a lion tamer who has to be hyper-vigilant and is always straining to maintain control. She tries to be firm but her nurturing side gets the upper hand more than it should. Dad complains that she is not tough enough. If she would only crack down on Junior's behavior, he would come under control. After all, Dad points out, "Junior never pulls those shenanigans with me." Mom, however, doesn't buy this. She believes that Dad uses terrorist tactics to control Junior. In fact, she tries to run interference between Dad and Junior because she thinks Dad is harsh and even cruel. Dad complains that Mom undermines his disciplinary authority. Mom says that she is afraid of Dad's bad temper and that he might hurt Junior. The scenario goes on and on.

By the time Junior enters school, the problem can no longer be ignored. Junior's distractibility and impulsive behavior begin to drive his teacher over-the-edge as well. The school calls a conference to discuss Junior's behavior. The school suggests that the parents consult with their family physician. The physician diagnoses Junior with ADHD and puts him on Ritalin or some other medication. The scenario goes on and on.

Although the medication has a somewhat calming effect, Junior's behavior is still erratic and he seems to experience mood swings as well. Finally, it is recommended that Mom and Dad refer Junior to a mental health professional. Mom is willing to follow this recommendation. However, Dad views this as being totally unnecessary. "What!" Dad yells. "My son is not crazy. What does he need to go to a head-shrinker for? If you (Mom) would just crack down, there wouldn't' be any problem."

Mom and Dad obviously have different views about Junior's behavior, how he should be reared, and who is responsible for the problem. The so called working together "team approach" never existed in the first place. Mom and Dad lack parenting skills. But most importantly, they virtually cannot communicate with each other. How can they, therefore, be expected to successfully work with Junior.

With the passage of time, Junior becomes a master at manipulating his parents. He becomes particularly adept in applying the "divide and conquer" principle in order to get his way. When Dad disciplines him, he fusses and complains to Mom. She then gets on Dad's case. After the fight, Junior often gets what he wanted. By now, Dad is in the habit of blowing up and Mom is forever trying to do her best to keep a lid on Dad's increasing volatility. And when Junior's sister was born, this hardly helped the situation. Junior and his sister fight constantly. She does well in school, has friends, and is helpful around the house. Because Junior is frustrated with himself and envious, he repeatedly picks on his sister. This only adds to the strain that Mom and Dad are experiencing. Without professional intervention to fuse "the team" together, the marriage is headed for disaster.

How is that something that began so good can turn out so bad? Sometimes we get blind-sided by life. A challenge, such as rearing an ADHD child, becomes thrust upon us. And we may not have the training or personality reserves to adequately cope with this. We sometimes ignore or forget that parenting is a team effort and that the contribution of both parents is essential to the emotional and social well-being of the child. We lose sight of the fact that the preservation of our marriage might be the most important factor in successfully rearing our children. As a result, we may fail to listen, to understand,

and to nurture that which brought us together in the first place. If this goes on too long, hurt feelings, mistrust, increasing resentment, and even rage toward each other replace the love and commitment that were once so prominent in the relationship. Divorce and all the hazards surrounding this then follows.

An associate of mine once said, "The best gift you can give a child is a good marriage." I didn't stop to think about this at the time. But over the years, I have come to appreciate the wisdom that this simple sentence conveys. Unfortunately, in our day and age this goal is not easily achieved, particularly when an ADHD child becomes a member of the family. While the ADHD child is not responsible for a parental breakup, the task of rearing him or her can be an onerous one. Being able to work well together can go a long way in successfully achieving this task. Parents need to take the time to exert the necessary energy in nurturing their existing marriages if this is at all possible. Fusing together "a team effort" after the breakup is necessary for helping the ADHD child to cope with his or her already difficult situation. Hopefully, however, this can be accomplished before, not after the marriage is dissolved.

NOTE

1. Guy R. Lefrancois, *The Lifespan* (Belmont, CA: Wadsworth Publishing Co., 1999), 282–285.

Chapter Thirteen

The Acquisition of Confidence: How Important Is This?

In an article by Janet Polivy and Peter C. Herman, the importance of confidence in achieving success was focused upon.[1] The authors cited several examples of current research that was conducted between the years of 1995 and 1999. The results clearly indicated that higher self-efficacy or confidence in oneself made a significant difference between success and failure. In summing up their findings, Polivy and Herman contended that persons who believe that they will succeed are more likely to do so. This occurs for two reasons. First, those who believe that they can succeed are more likely to make the effort. And second, confident persons are more likely to persist when adversity arrives. Because persistence can be a critical component in overcoming adversities, having confidence is of the utmost importance in achieving success. In conclusion, Polivy and Herman noted there was a considerable body of evidence that higher self-efficacy scores and confidence were associated with successful outcomes in a variety of the programs that were studied.

Common sense tells us that the belief or lack of belief in oneself is one of the central ingredients upon which human motivation is founded. If a person has confidence, it makes sense that he or she is more likely to exert the effort in the pursuit of socially desirable goals. On the other hand, if a person views him or herself as being incapable of achieving these goals, then little or not efforts is likely to be put forth. In case of the latter, directing one's energy into other areas, which may not be socially desirable, would be much more likely to occur.

Let's put the preceding into a more practical context. All of us want our young people to pursue goals that prepare them to be viable, upright members of the community. The pursuit of a good education; acquiring recognition for successful achievement in the arts, sciences, and humanities; and the development of athletic skills are areas in which we would like our youngsters to excel. Building good work habits, developing hands on technical and mechanical competence, and learning social skills for appropriately interfacing with other people are also laudable goals that we want our children to acquire in their most formative years. However, whether our young people are willing to put forth the necessary effort to achieve these depends on how they perceive themselves and their ability to accomplish such goals. If a child believes that he is a "loser," a "retard," or just plain "dumb," it is unlikely that he will try to achieve any of the above. The pursuit of these goals would, from the child's perspective, require too much time, energy, and persistence. And from the child's point of view, his or her efforts would likely be unsuccessful anyway. So what would be the point of trying? Why would he or she want to make life more difficult than it already happens to be? The youngster, therefore, might be more likely to pursue more immediate, short-term goals, even if these were considered to be undesirable from the adult's point of view.

For example, most young people want to be recognized by their peers for being good at something. Unfortunately, some children have given up hope that they could ever achieve positive recognition from their parents and teachers. As a result, they take great pride in being antagonists. They behave rebelliously in the face of adult authority, and they mock the educational process by becoming class clowns and social misfits. While such behavior is considered to be counterproductive from the adult perspective, the antagonistic youngster views this quite differently. As indicated previously, in the child's mind being "bad" is good. Why? The answer is quite simple. The antagonist is often recognized as being humorous and even "cool" by his classmates. Peers laugh at the "bad" youngster's jibes at his classroom teacher. His bravado and contempt for authority are worn like a badge of courage for all to see. Some secretly admire the antagonist's twisted notion of bravery, even though they would hardly dare to engage in this outrageous behavior themselves. They clearly recognize that they would have much to lose by behaving so badly. However, deep down inside many really admire the "rebel without a cause" and wish they could be like him. After all, being perceived as being "cool" and "in control" are attractive qualities to a child or adolescent. And all of this recognition can be acquired almost instantly. One does not have to engage in long periods of hard work or give up short-term pleasures that can make life so much fun at the present moment. This is what makes outrageous behavior so attractive. It can lead to immediately beneficial results, and it requires very little substantial effort. The child or adolescent simply has to behave in an obnoxious fashion, and for some, this is a relatively easy task.

While there are many reasons why youngsters engage in self-defeating behavior, the root of the problem often stems from a lack of confidence. Rather than take the risk of competing against others or looking foolish, they engage in antisocial acts and gravitate toward those activities that provide them with immediate pleasure or instant gratification. This lack of faith in themselves, in other people, and in life itself is like an unchecked cancer. If left untreated, it devours the living cells of an otherwise potentially good and viable personality.

If we think about the preceding, this has far reaching implications in determining the kinds of habits, which can become deeply embedded into our personality structure with the passage of time. People who lack confidence are much more likely "to grab the brass ring now." Even though brass tarnishes quickly and leaves a green stain on one's finger, the brass ring glitters at least for a moment. Bad habits are like the glittering brass ring. Whether it is drug or alcohol abuse, promiscuity, over-eating, or the explosive reaction to a minor irritant, these provide one with immediate and intense pleasure, relief, or temporary satisfactions. And there is one thing of which we can be certain. Such maladaptive behavior patterns do not simply come about by chance. There are causes that bring these about. The trick is to identify and gain conscious control of these so that we can live more productive and happier lives. A lack of confidence is one of these major causes.

Most assuredly, the genesis of many of our adult problems began in childhood. Dashed hopes, broken dreams, and the loss of believing that our sustained efforts could ever amount to anything may have plagued many of us during our youthful years. A lack of self-confidence may have caused some of us to sell ourselves short. As a result, we might have made poor choices that have a profoundly negative impact on the way in which we live our lives today. How many times have we heard older people say, "I'd like to live my life over again with what I know today." It is sad but true. The reality is that many adults discover potentials within themselves that, if these had been recognized and nurtured earlier, could have led to a much more satisfying and fulfilling life.

However, during their most formative years, they lacked a belief in themselves and their ability to be successful. Instead, a jaded version of who they were and what they could achieve led to "grabbing the brass ring" too early in their tumultuous youthful years.

So the question still remains. Just how important is the acquisition of self-confidence. It is probably the most important aspect of the child's developing personality. No matter how talented a person may be, the actualization of that talent will not occur if he or she lacks the confidence to develop it. The development of self-confidence must be undertaken during the youngster's most formative years before the challenges of living become increasingly more complex and compelling. For the parents of ADHD children, fostering the development of confidence should not be left to chance. Our ADHD youngsters are particularly vulnerable in this regard. They are more likely than most of their peers to lack confidence in themselves. It is important, therefore, that we attempt to correct this deficiency as soon as possible. More on this topic will be presented in the next chapter.

NOTE

1. Janet Polivy and Peter C. Herman, "If At First You Don't Succeed: False Hopes of Self-Change" *American Psychologist* 57, no.9 (September 2002): 677–689.

Chapter Fourteen

The Rudiments of Building Confidence

Building self-confidence does not come about effortlessly or easily. Like the development of any worthwhile personality trait, the acquisition of confidence requires hard and sustained work. The psychological literature shows that real self-confidence is earned.[1,2,3] This means that the child must engage in challenging activities and succeed in accomplishing them. Such success proves to the youngster that he or she can perform competently when the effort is made to do so.

Simply telling a child that he or she has the ability to perform successfully is unlikely to enhance his or her confidence. No matter how many times we tell a youngster how competent he or she could be, this alone will not improve the child's self-image. Rather, it is the actual accomplishment of challenging tasks that leads to the development of confidence. When the child masters a task or overcomes some adversity, this provides real life verification that he or she can perform successfully. In other words, the results of the child's behavior provide direct feedback indicating that he can actually do something that he may have doubted that he could do before.

The acquisition of self-confidence begins slowly, laboriously, and in small increments. It does not come about all at once. The children's story entitled *The Little Engine That Could* is a good example of this.[4] If you have read the story, you will recall that the larger and more powerful engines that preceded the little engine looked on the upcoming hill that they had to climb with great trepidation. They lacked confidence in their ability to accomplish this task, and therefore, made no effort to even try. The Little Engine also looked at the hill and experienced these same feelings. However, instead of allowing his fear of failure to get the better of him, he decided that he would make the effort to reach the top. While the larger engines snickered at his audacity, the

Little Engine began his ascent. Each small gain prompted him to say to himself, "I think I can." Each chug of his engine and each piece of the track that he ascended led to more confidence. The "I think I can; I think I can" thoughts increased in their momentum and intensity as The Little Engine began to successfully move up the hill. By the time that The Little Engine approached the summit, the "I think I can" thoughts were being generated so rapidly, forthrightly, and convincingly that it was evident that nothing was going to stop him from reaching his goal. The Little Engine had acquired self-confidence. He earned this sought after prize by facing and overcoming the hill, not all at once, but by moving forward one small step at a time. Each small success proved to him that he had the ability to make it to the top. Even his more powerful peers, who were actually better equipped for this task, were unable to achieve this. Despite their talent, they lacked the central ingredient that is essential to all success, the belief in their ability to do it.

While *The Little Engine That Could* is a child's story, there is much wisdom in its contents. True self-confidence only comes about by mastering life's challenges, one task at a time. Encouraging our children to make use of their abilities and to face adversity is of paramount importance. Teaching them to overcome the fear of sleeping in a dark room; encouraging them to share their opinions in a classroom discussion; insisting that they properly complete family chores; requiring that they behave in a mannerly and civil fashion; and learning to dress and groom themselves appropriately are the little and seemingly unimportant tasks that, if mastered, begin to develop self-confidence. None of the preceding tasks are fun. It requires self-discipline to do these properly day in and day out. It is these small responsibilities and the mastery of them that lay the groundwork for being able to confidently face the bigger challenges that are yet to come. Ultimately, we want our despondent ADHD children to be able to convincingly say to themselves, "I think I can." Most importantly, however, we want them to really believe it.

NOTES

1. Paul Lavin and Kathryn Lavin, *A Comprehensive Guide for Parenting the ADHD Child* (Baltimore, MD: Publish America), 20–22.

2. Paul Lavin and Kathryn Lavin, *A Comprehensive Guide*, 78–91.

3. Janet Polivy and Peter C. Herman, "If At First You Don't Succeed: False Hopes of Self-Change" *American Psychologist* 57, no.9 (September 2002): 677–689.

4. Watty Piper, *The Little Engine That Could* (New York: Platt & Munk Publishers, 2002).

Chapter Fifteen

Affective Education: A Necessary Ingredient for Helping ADHD Children to Cope with Depression

Affective education is an important component for helping ADHD children in understanding and coping with depression. As noted previously, ADHD children, particularly in their most formative years, have difficulty labeling their emotions and the thoughts associated with them. It is affective education that can play a key role in correcting this deficit. Moreover, it is affective education that can provide the child with the skills that are necessary for coping with those negative emotions, which can become self-destructive if not properly understood and mastered.

It is important to note that affective education is often confused with character education, social skills training, or other forms of education focusing on values and responsible behavior. The definition of affect, according to Webster,[1] embraces three components: (1) "feeling"; (2) "the conscious, subjective aspects of an emotion"; and (3) "to act upon (as a person) on his mind or in his feelings to affect a response." In light of this definition, therefore, any program that emphasizes affective education should focus upon the understanding of feelings and those factors that influence them.

It should be kept in mind that the way a person feels can have a marked impact on how he or she behaves. The more intense the feeling, the stronger will be the reaction to it. If a person's feelings become overly intense, this could lead to explosive or even self-destructive behavior. This is why acquiring a knowledge of our emotions and those dynamics that affect them is so important. Understanding "the conscious, subjective aspects of an emotion," as Webster indicates, is essential in acquiring self-control, a most important attribute for achieving social, professional, and academic success. Misunderstood, unrecognized, and unbridled emotion can easily lead to chaos and serious trouble for those who lose control and those who are the victims of this.

53

With the preceding in mind, it only makes sense to provide ADHD children with an affective education program. After all, ADHD children have experienced far more negative emotional intensity than their more fortunate peers who have not been afflicted with this disorder. Many ADHD youngsters have been emotionally battered and bruised for many years. Their nerves have become like an open wound that continues to fester and never heals. And the worst part of this is that peers and even adults intentionally or inadvertently rub salt into it.

It's no wonder that these unfortunate young people over-react with so much frequency. They are forever in pain anyway, and those around them only exacerbate this with ridicule, teasing, and unkind comments. As a result, ADHD children often experience intense mood swings. They behave like impulsively driven jumping jacks in response to even well-meaning and constructive criticism from sincere and caring people.

Obviously, if ADHD youngsters remain in such an emotionally encumbered state, their prospects for a successful future will diminish with the passage of time. In order to help correct this, an affective education program must be devised and put into practice. The assumptions on which such a program is based is that our perceptions (our view of things) are responsible for the way that we feel about ourselves, other people, and life itself. If our views are negative, then a steady diet of depression, anger, anxiety, and frustration will continually fill our emotional plate. Such a combination of affective negativity can only result in irritable, oppositional, and even antisocial behavior. Moreover, the child's perception of him or herself will be a poor one. A dislike or hatred of oneself mutilates the youngster's self-concept and negativity impacts on every facet of his or her life. It is an intense dislike of oneself that leads to the marked sadness, depression, and even despair that was referred to earlier. Who in their right mind would try to face life's challenges believing that they were incapable and that their efforts would only lead to failure?

As emphasized previously, it is the erroneous ADHD child's perceptions that need to be corrected if better emotional control and the self-mastery associated with this are to be attained. Whether we are aware of this or not, our perceptions consist of actual words and sentences that we say to ourselves. In some cases, these thoughts are so automatically programmed within us that we don't even realize that such self-talk is taking place. However, it is the language mediators, the way we subjectively define our experiences, which determine how we feel about the world around us. This is the heart and soul of affective education. It is specifically designed to teach our children to label their emotions and to control these by engaging in "right thinking." An ADHD child's altered perceptions in combination with the learning of better coping skills can make all the differences in helping him or her to face life's challenges with optimism and self-confidence.

This author has put together an inexpensive and complete affective education program that parents, educators, and mental health professionals can use with ADHD children.[2] This, in conjunction with self-control training games[3] and children's literature,[4] can be particularly beneficial in helping the ADHD child to label his or her affect, its varying levels of intensity, and how this effects his or her behavior. For example, the youngster is taught to label a specific emotion such as anger. He or she is then taught that the feeling of anger can vary in its intensity ranging from being annoyed to outright rage or fury. The latter can obviously lead to behavioral over-reactions. The former, however, can be a motivating catalyst for taking proper corrective action to solve the problem. The annoyed person still has his or her reasoning power in tact. He or she is, therefore, able to weigh sensible alternatives and make a strategic plan, which can then be put into practice. Unlike the furious person, he or she is much more likely to maintain his or her objectivity and to behave in a fashion that will produce a successful outcome.

As stressed previously, a good affective education program helps the child to replace affective negativity with hopefulness and self-confidence. An optimistic, emotionally secure ADHD youngster is far more likely to control and manage his or her ADHD than a morose, frustrated, and angry ADHD child who has given up on trying to behave successfully.

NOTES

1. Frederick C. Mish, ed., *Webster's Ninth New Collegiate Dictionary* (Springfield, MA: Merriam-Webster, 1984), 61.

2. Paul Lavin and Kathryn Lavin, *Koping for Kids: A Coping Skills Program for Elementary School Children* (Minneapolis, MN: Educational Media Corp, 2005), 23–30.

3. Paul Lavin and Kathryn Lavin, *A Comprehensive Guide for Parenting the ADHD Child* (Baltimore, MD: Publish America, 2005), 99–115

4. Paul Lavin and Kathryn Lavin, *A Comprehensive Guide*, 116–139.

Chapter Sixteen

Developing an Internal Locus of Control: The Antidote to Hopelessness

The research on the importance of developing an internal locus of control goes all the way back to 1965. In a study conducted by Crandall and her associates, the results showed that children who did well academically attributed their success or failure to their own efforts. Children who did poorly, on the other hand, believed that luck, fate, other people, or environmental circumstances were responsible for whether they succeeded or failed.[1] A number of years passed before other studies were conducted that supported Crandall's findings.[2] Researchers confirmed that an internal locus of control was formed by the long standing beliefs that children hold about themselves based on their past history of success or failure. Again, children who were successful were likely to develop an internal locus of control. Children with a history of failure, however, were much more likely to perceive themselves as being incompetent and manipulated and dominated by those environmental circumstances surrounding them. Hence, an external rather than an internal locus of control governed their feelings and actions.

Whether the youngster develops an internal or external locus of control can have far reaching effects on how he or she behaves when confronted with challenging tasks. A child's belief can serve as a self-fulfilling prophecy. The thoughts and feelings that the youngster experiences at that moment in time can have a marked impact on whether he or she makes a concerted effort to master a task or withdraws, acts out, or refuses to try. The child who quits trying may actually have the ability to perform successfully. However, if he or she expects to fail, a substandard or poor performance is likely to follow, despite the fact that the child may have the skill to succeed.

It is these antecedent thoughts and feelings that children bring to the situation that can ultimately determine success or failure. As emphasized previously, if children perceive themselves as being incompetent, this view would impact on how they feel. And it is their emotional state, how they feel at the moment, which will influence whether they are motivated to make the needed effort to succeed. For example, a child might believe the following: "I am a stupid person who never does anything right." Any child who believes this about himself is likely to feel highly anxious and experience marked feelings of futility and hopelessness. On the other hand, the youngster who has a positive view of his or her capabilities is much more likely to be optimistic about the prospects for achieving success when confronted with new and challenging tasks.

It should be noted that children whose views are negative are much more likely to perceive themselves as being the victims of unfair circumstances as well. Moreover, they are more likely to perceive themselves as being disliked and that teachers assign tasks to them beyond their capability. Because of these beliefs, such children are quick to blame or to look for excuses to explain away their lack of effort or failure. Hence, an external rather than an internal locus of control is formed. Unfortunately, this habitual way of thinking becomes more deeply embedded into the child's personality with the passage of time and the continued repetition of one failure after another. Unless this cycle becomes altered, such externalizing and the avoidance of taking responsibility for one's actions can become a rigid, stubborn trait, which is not easily changed.

Blaming, excuse making, and defensiveness may take away the emotional pain of facing and coping with the negative consequences of one's actions. Moreover, such behavior enables the child to avoid the responsibility of making those needed changes in order to improve his or her performance. While such an avoidance may make the child feel better for the moment, it only strengthens the negative thoughts and feelings that he or she has about him or herself. The continuation of bad habits, negative thinking, and the hopeless feelings associated with these can only further erode the youngster's already poor self-concept. How can a child develop a positive view of himself and the needed self-confidence to perform successfully if such behavior remains unaltered?

In light of the preceding, one can easily see why depression would undermine the child's willingness to make the necessary effort to succeed. Depressed children don't try. Rather, they quit easily, believing that their efforts will be hopeless. Being an ADHD child only compounds the problem. ADHD children must not only learn to cope with the symptoms of this disorder, but they must make the effort to overcome the discouragement that is associated with this as well. This can be a "double whammy," which is not easily reconciled with children who already believe that the odds are heavily stacked against them.

Despite this difficulty, helping the ADHD child to develop an internal locus of control is essential to overcoming a poor self-concept. If the youngster can learn to think positively instead of negatively, then his or her debilitating emotional state can be modified accordingly. Such an emotional uplifting will energize the child and provide him or her with the motivation to make the needed effort to perform successfully. Once this occurs, repeated success will follow. This then can lead to the development of an internal locus of control. The mental connection between the youngster's efforts and the positive consequences flowing from this can be made. And with the passage of time and continued success, this connection will deepen, eventually creating a permanently more positive change in the child's perceptions and the feelings generated by them. Hopefulness can then replace depression and the inertia associated with this. This makes it far more likely that the ADHD child's future will be both a promising and productive one.

NOTES

1. Paul Lavin, *Parenting the Over-Active Child* (Lanham, MD: Madison Books, 1989), 151.
2. Sam Goldstein and Michael Goldstein, *Managing Attention Disorders in Children* (New York: John Wiley & Sons, 1990), 280–281.

Chapter Seventeen

Teaching the ADHD Child to Develop an Internal Locus of Control

As emphasized previously, a most important attribute in achieving self-confidence is the acquisition of an internal locus of control. Persons with an external locus of control believe that they are directly responsible for the consequences of their actions. It is not fate, luck, other people, or circumstances that determine what happens to them. Rather, the choices that they make and their actions following from these lead to the pleasant or unpleasant consequences of which they are the recipients.[1,2]

The preceding applies to adults as well as children. The research shows that persons who are successful connect their actions to what follows. On the other hand, if they do poorly, they put the blame for this squarely on their shoulders without making excuses.

The acquisition of an internal locus of control and the self-confidence associated with this is particularly important for children diagnosed with ADHD. Because they have difficulty controlling their bodies, attending to task, and curbing their impulsivity, it is easy for them to conclude that there is little that they can do to cope with their condition. Perceiving themselves as the victims of "bad genes," unfair criticism, and an inherited over-active nervous system can generate considerable self-pity and strong feelings of powerlessness. The root of the latter can lead to a profound and chronic depression that plagues the child from one day to the next. Depression and hopelessness go hand in hand. The child's behavior is driven by the perception that "What I do won't make any difference, so why make the effort." The frustration, acting-out, and belligerence that we observe actually "spin off" from this self-defeating thinking and the negative emotionality associated with it.

In order to help ADHD children to develop an internal locus of control, a proper environmental structure must be put into place. The earlier that this can occur the better. The purpose of this structure would be to teach the child that his or her behavior causes success or failure. In order to achieve this objective, two things must be taught. First, if the youngster chooses to behave appropriately, positive consequences will follow. And second, if he or she makes poor choices, the consequences following these will be negative. For example, Robert is taught that if he puts his hand on a hot stove, his hand will be burned. It is important for Robert to be specifically instructed in understanding that his decision to touch the stove causes the pain. The stove does not choose to burn Robert. In other words, Robert's decision to place his hand on the hot stove is the cause for the burn. Because the stove is incapable of making choices and acting on its own free will, it cannot be held responsible for inflicting pain. Rather, Robert, by making a bad choice, inflicted the pain on himself. Again, it is Robert's decision to touch the stove that caused the negative consequences.

The message that is being conveyed in this example is clear enough. Robert is taught that if he thinks before acting, unnecessary unpleasantness can be avoided. Parents, educators, and mental health professionals who work with ADHD children can use such everyday examples to point out the cause and effect relationships between the choices that we make and the consequences that follow from them.

Instructions such as the preceding not only help ADHD children to learn to curb their tendency to behave impulsively, but it also provides the foundation upon which good planning, the anticipation of consequences, and good self-control can be built. Using this approach teaches the ADHD child to think about the impending results of his or her behavior before it occurs. Such instruction then trains him or her to make the mental connection between the choice, the action itself, and the actual outcome. And it is this connection, which is repeatedly made over the course of time, that leads to the development of an internal locus of control and the belief that "What I do can make a difference."

Again, it must be stressed that the earlier such training begins the better. Because ADHD children have much difficulty concentrating and staying on task, they particularly require more specific, clear, and forthright instruction than their non-ADHD peers. ADHD children who are able to grasp the preceding are far less likely to become depressed. They can learn that they have the power to alter their own lives. Their ADHD symptoms may still remain. However, the confidence that they can do something to control these is the antidote for those depressive feelings, which can seriously undermine their motivation to make the effort to do so.

It is important to recognize that throughout the course of each day, there are numerous situations in which the connection between choice, action, and consequence can be taught to the child. Whether the child learns this largely depends upon how we respond to the youngster's choices and the resulting behavior that follows these. When children engage in proper behavior, which leads to positive consequences, we need to immediately acknowledge this. Describing what the child did and the result of his or her actions need to be clearly specified.

For example, John puts his school materials in his book bag and then places it by the door in the evening. As a result, he is easily able to locate the book bag the next morning and leaves for school on time. This pleases John's parents because it helps them to get to work on time as well. In this example the parents might say, "John we would like to compliment you on organizing your school materials, putting them into the book bag, and placing the bag near the door last evening. Being ready the night before school helped us all leave on time. We are pleased because you helped to make the morning hassle free and much more pleasant." Note that in this example the parents first compliment John in preparation for the positive message that they are about to impart. They then specify the behaviors, ("Your book bag was organized in advance and you placed it next to the door.") and the consequences attached to them, ("This helped us all to leave on time and made the morning hassle free and more pleasant").

The preceding model can be applied to many other situations throughout the day. Unless the child has an emotional ax to grind with the persons who deliver such messages, he or she should be receptive to this information. With continued repetition, the needed mental connection between choice, behavior, and outcome will be made, particularly if the child's relationship with the parents is a positive one. After all, most children want to please their parents. Providing them with insight on how they can do so can only be beneficial.

Even behavior that leads to negative consequences can be instructive if presented properly. For instance, let's use the previous example to make this point. John does not pack his book bag the night before going to school. Instead the bag and school materials are scattered about the house. The next morning John has trouble locating the bag and the materials. It takes a good deal of extra time to find them and to pack the bag. As a result, the parents nag John because they are anxious about leaving on time. John, in return argues that his parents are rushing him. John is late for school and his parents are late for work.

John's parents might address this problem with him as follows, "John, we need to talk with you about a situation that is causing unpleasantness for all of us. You have not been packing your book bag the night before school. The bag and school materials are scattered about the house. In the morning, you have to spend extra time locating the materials and finding the bag and packing it. This causes us to get anxious because we don't want to be late for work and we don't want you to be late for school. We then wind up nagging and you argue with us. This is unpleasant for all of us and it starts the day off on a bad note." Again, in this example the parents set the tone by pointing out that they want to talk about the situation, which is "unpleasant" for everyone. They clearly specify that the failure to behave properly is the cause of the problem ("You are not packing your book bag the night before school. The bag and the materials are scattered about the house. In the morning, you have to spend extra time locating the materials and finding the bag and packing it."). The negative consequences are: "This causes us to be anxious because we don't want to be late for work and we don't want you to be late for school. Moreover, we wind up nagging and you argue with us. This is unpleasant and starts the day off on a bad note." Again, unless the youngster is angry with his or her parents for some unknown reason and is attempting to engage in a "power struggle," the mental connection between his or her behavior and the consequences associated with it should be easily made. The child can learn that he or she is far from being powerless. Rather, his or her actions can have a profound influence on what happens to him or her or those persons within their surroundings.

In order to firmly fix the connection between action and consequences in the child's mind, the application of behavior modification principles can be very helpful. The central premise upon which this approach is founded is simple enough. That which follows a behavior determines whether that behavior is learned and whether it will be continued or discontinued in the future. If pleasant consequences follow a behavior, this increases the likelihood that it will continue. On the other hand, if unpleasant consequences follow that behavior, it is much more likely to cease in order to avoid the unpleasantness associated with it. It should be noted that consequences can serve as powerful motivators. They can have a profound influence on whether the child is willing to exert the necessary physical, emotional, and intellectual effort to learn. It is up to parents, educators, and mental health professionals who work with ADHD children to identify and arrange these contingencies accordingly so that this can occur.

While the preceding focuses mainly on the child's actions and their outcomes, it should be noted that cognitive, as well as behavioral changes occur by properly applying behavior modification principles. In other words, changes in the child's thinking about himself and his ability to influence what happens to him can be the by products of such a program. The youngster makes the mental connection between "what I do" and the positive or negative outcomes that result from this. For example, Sarah's parents tell her that if she satisfactorily completes all home and school responsibilities for one week, they will take her and a friend out for pizza. Because Sarah is motivated, she successfully fulfills all of her responsibilities. Her parents then take Sarah and her friend to a restaurant and they are able to order a pizza of their choice. The cognitive connection that would be made by Sarah is as follows: "Because I satisfactorily completed my home and school obligations, I earned the privilege of going out for a pizza with my friend. My behavior was responsible for earning this privilege. It was not luck or other people that earned this privilege for me. I earned it by my own efforts."

It should be emphasized that arranging environmental contingencies so that the ADHD child can earn rewards for good behavior can encourage better choice making, leading to increased success. The more success that the child experiences, the more likely it is that he or she will make the connection between "my behavior and the results that follow." Furthermore, the youngster whose actions repeatedly lead to success will become more self-confident. And it is self-confidence, the belief that, "What I do influences what happens to me," that is the bedrock upon which an internal locus of control is founded. As stressed previously, this is the antidote for overcoming depression, which all too often hinders the ADHD child's potential for progress. More on constructing a behavior modification program for the purpose of helping ADHD children to develop an internal locus of control will be presented in a later chapter.

Finally, it should be noted that poor choice making and inappropriate behavior should be followed by unpleasant consequences. These must be of sufficient duration and intensity so that the ADHD child learns from his or her mistakes and is motivated to make better choices and to act more appropriately in the future. For instance, Sarah fails to fulfill her home and school obligations for the week. As a result, she is grounded for the entire weekend and loses all privileges. Provided that there are no emotional impediments interfering with Sarah's ability to learn from her mistakes, the following cognitive connection between her behavior and the loss of weekend privileges can be made: "Because I failed to fulfill my home and school responsibilities, I have been grounded and lost all of my privileges for the weekend. My failure to act properly caused this to happen. If I fulfill my obligations at home and school, then I can avoid being grounded and my privileges for the next weekend will be restored. It was not luck or other people that were responsible for what happened to me. It was my lack of effort that brought this about."

As emphasized previously, an ADHD child who is emotionally encumbered by angry and vengeful feelings may not make the connection between his or her behavior and the resulting consequences. In some "hard core" cases, children may actually not care about the negative impact of their actions. Their bad behavior might be an attempt to inflict punishment upon those adults who they believe have treated them unfairly. And this attitude can generalize to all adults, even though some may be sincerely caring and trying to be helpful to them. When children have an emotional ax to grind, they are not likely to make those cognitive connections, which have been referred to earlier. They are unlikely to give credence to the later statement in the previous example ("It was not luck or other people that were responsible for what happened to me. It was my lack of effort that brought this about."). Instead, the opposite, an external locus of control, forms in the child's mind. Luck, fate, environmental circumstances, or other people are blamed for the problem.

In light of the preceding, it is imperative that those emotional issues, which are impeding the child's progress, be identified and addressed. Once this is accomplished, it is far more likely that a plan for fostering an internal locus of control and the self-confidence associated with this can be developed and successfully put into practice. Time, patience, and persistence in the pursuit of this goal will pay rich dividends to those parents, educators, and mental health professionals who keep this in mind and make the concerted effort to bring this about.

NOTES

1. Paul Lavin and Kathryn Lavin, *A Comprehensive Guide for Parenting the ADHD Child* (Baltimore, MD: Publish America, 2005), 20–23.
2. Sam Goldstein and Michael Goldstein, *Managing Attention Disorders in Children* (New York: John Wiley & Sons, 1990), 280–281.

Chapter Eighteen

Strength Identification: The Building Block Upon Which Hope Is Founded

As noted earlier, ADHD children are frequently plummeted with negative feedback, which has an eroding effect on their self-concept. Because their self-perception is a poor one, they fail to recognize their positive qualities, believing that they are inept in all facets of their lives. Such a "global condemnation" of their personality, which can become a deeply embedded view, is difficult to change. Their often fixed, negative self-concept fuels an unending feeling of hopelessness. It is this that must be altered so that they will be willing to invest the necessary cognitive and emotional energy in order to function successfully.

A major step in the quest for building hope rests on identifying specific strengths that the ADHD child possesses. The identification of these strengths can be gleaned from observations of the child's behavior, his or her records, and the school file. Written reports, test scores, and descriptions of the child's strong points submitted by parents, teachers, and other adults can be presented in such a way that the youngster will be unable to deny that these strengths have a solid foundation in reality.

An example on how this can be done is as follows. The school records usually contain information on teacher observations of the child's behavior and his or her scores on various educational tests and tests of intelligence. An examination of the latter can be particularly fruitful in strength identification. For instance, many ADHD children have taken intelligence tests such as the Wechsler Intelligence Scale for Children. Within these tests, there are various subtests, which measure specific abilities. On the Wechsler test, for example, there is a subtest called Block Design. The child is asked to assemble red and white blocks so that they match a design, which is presented on a stimulus card. Block Design measures perceptual-motor capability. A child who does well on this task may have good mechanical aptitude.

Let's suppose that a youngster achieved a standard score of 14 on this sub-test. This would mean that he or she scored at the 91st percentile, performing better than 90 out of 100 persons who had previously taken this test. Pointing this out to a depressed ADHD child can be a true "eye opener" and could have a salutary effect on his or her emotional state. The following might be said to the youngster: "On this subtest you did better than 90 out of 100 students who previously took this test. In fact, out of 1,000 children who had previously taken this test, you actually did better than 900 of them. This places you in the Superior Range and shows that you may have excellent mechanical capability. Engineers, designers, mechanics, computer repair technicians, architects, and builders have ability like yours. You can see this score right here in your records (point to the score). This is not something that I'm making up. What do you think about that?" By asking the latter question, you can assess whether the youngster grasps what you are saying and whether further explanation is needed to make your point.

Providing such information and asking the child to evaluate this can have a catalytic effect in getting the youngster to revise his view of himself. This could open the door to exploration of a career choice and help to foster the beginning of a dream for the future. Such an approach can be a real antidote for the elimination of hopelessness. Of course in the preceding example, the person who is interpreting the records would have to be trained in understanding what the specific test measures, the meaning of standard scores and percentiles, and how these can be presented to those individuals who are inexperienced in this area. School counselors, psychologists, and most teachers who have taken courses on educational tests and measurement can be helpful to parents in this regard. They can instruct parents on the meaning of these scores and how these can be productively conveyed to their offspring. Moreover, educational and mental health professionals can point out these scores to the ADHD children with whom they work and encourage them to make good use of their talents.

Besides using the records, a keen observer can identify various strengths based on how the ADHD child behaves in different situations. Keep in mind that ADHD children often score average to above average on tests of intelligence. Besides being intelligent and energetic (the latter can be a positive trait), many ADHD children have athletic, musical, theatrical, and artistic capabilities. ADHD children are often fearless risk takers. While this can be potentially dangerous, it could also be interpreted as having "courage," provided that such risk is initiated and sustained within a socially acceptable framework.

While being an ADHD child has its drawbacks, some adults believe that having ADHD was responsible for helping them to be successful. For instance, it was reported that David Neeleman, founder of Jet Blue Airlines, credits his creativity and "out of the box" thinking and passion for success to his ADHD.[1] Thom Hartman, author of *The Edison Gene: ADHD and the Gift of the Hunter Child*, contends that people with ADHD "may instead be our most creative individuals, our most extraordinary thinkers, our most brilliant inventors and pioneers."[2,3] In fact, there has been a spate of books that point to the positive aspects of ADHD such as *Delivered From Distraction: Getting the Most Out of Life with Attention Deficit Disorder*, by Doctors Edward Hallowell and John Ritey and *The Gift of ADHD* by Laura Honos-Webb.[4,5]

As one can see, ADHD and the characteristics associated with it can be considered to be positive as well as negative depending on how we view them. ADHD children typically perceive this disorder in a most negative and debilitating light. They often see themselves as being totally "bad" with a hopeless orientation for the future. It's no wonder that they often become Oppositional Defiant and Conduct Disordered (antisocial) as they pass into the adolescent and adulthood years. It is the identification of strengths and the conviction that these can be developed successfully, which can inspire ADHD children to channel their energy into socially appropriate areas. A thorough strength assessment and communicating these to the ADHD child is critical in motivating him or her toward the acquisition of an internal locus of control. As noted earlier, this is a true antidote for combating depression and should be programmed into the ADHD child's treatment plan.

NOTES

1. Marilyn Lewis, "The Upside of ADHD," *MSN Health & Fitness*, http://health.msn.com/centers/adhd/articlepage.aspx?cp-documented=100109339 (6, April 2006).
2. Marilyn Lewis, "The Upside of ADHD," 2.
3. Thom Hartman, *The Edison Gene: ADHD and the Gift of the Hunter Child* (Rochester, VT: Park Street Press, 2003).
4. Edward Hallowell and John Riley, *Delivered From Distraction: Getting the Most Out of Life with Attention Deficit Disorder* (New York: Touchstone, 1994).
5. Lara Honos-Webb, *The Gift of ADHD* (Oakland, CA: New Harbinger Publications, 2004).

Chapter Nineteen

Building A Behavior Modification Program for Rearing Children to Develop an Internal Locus of Control

A properly designed and implemented behavior modification program can be particularly effective in helping the ADHD child to develop an internal locus of control. As emphasized previously, it is the development of an internal locus of control which is the antidote for overcoming depression. The following principles should be taken into account in designing and putting into practice a behavior modification program in order to achieve this objective.[1,2]

1. Practically all behavior, whether it is good or bad, is learned. Parents can teach their children to behave appropriately or inappropriately. This depends on how they respond to their child's actions.
2. Behavior that is followed by positive consequences is likely to continue. Behavior that is followed by negative consequences is likely to stop.
3. The research shows that achievement oriented children are often generously rewarded with affection and attention by parents.[3] Although money, toys, and food can follow good behavior, thereby making it more likely that this will continue, children frequently seek praise. Thus, when parents follow good behavior with positive attention as well as material rewards, they actually strengthen that behavior. Parents should actually look for good behavior and reward it with praise as frequently as possible.
4. Children, whose good behavior is recognized and rewarded by their parents, develop good feelings about themselves. Because their parents emphasize positive behavior and encouragement, these children learn to expect to succeed. They learn that it is worth the time, effort, and commitment to try because success is always possible, even when the

odds are stacked against them. This is the basis upon which an internal locus of control is founded.

5. Children will not continue to engage in desirable behavior simply because their parents say it "ought" to be done or because their parents tell them to do it. Desirable behavior continues because the consequences are positive. Undesirable behavior terminates because the consequences are negative. Parents must apply the appropriate consequences to the right behavior. It is important not to inadvertently reward bad behavior or to penalize good behavior.

6. If behavior is undesirable, there are two ways to eliminate this. We can either ignore or punish the behavior. Keep in mind that behavior that is not followed by favorable consequences is likely to stop. If we cannot ignore bad behavior, however, it may have to be punished.

   When punishment is applied, it is important to make sure that the selected punishment fits the crime. For example, if Thomas steals money from his parents, it would make no sense to beat him and restrict him to his room for six months. Rather, the logical consequences would be to have Thomas repay the money or its equivalent in work time. In addition, Thomas should perform some extra work for the offended parent. This is required because of the inconvenience and disruption that Thomas caused for the entire family as a result of his antisocial behavior. Such a punishment is directly related to the act of stealing.

   The parents who punish in this manner are not being excessively harsh or engaging in "overkill." Remember, that excessive or harsh punishment leads to feelings of hopelessness and resentment within the child. Moreover, punishing the child with an "I-told-you-so" attitude only makes the child even more defensive. Such an atmosphere in the home is hardly conducive to teaching the child to develop an internal locus of control. As noted earlier, this leads to "power struggles" and vengeful behavior on the part of the child. The child, therefore, fails to learn from his or her mistakes.

   When a punishment is necessary, parents should indicate to the child that they are sorry that it must be administered. However, his or her behavior warranted it. This should be followed with encouragement to do better the next time.

7. Parental agreement on what constitutes desirable and undesirable behavior must be consistent and clearly communicated to the child. Disagreement between parents about expectations can cause negative feelings and confusion within the child. This is likely to lead to defensiveness and blaming rather than the development of an internal locus of control.

8. In order to facilitate the connection between the child's actions and consequences, having him or her actually verbalize (state in words) this connection should be stressed. If the youngster earns a privilege as a result of behaving positively, he or she should be taught to make the following statement: "I earned the privilege of (state the reward) because I (state the behavior that led to the reward)." For example, by going to bed on time during the week, James was given the privilege of staying up an extra hour on Friday and Saturday night. James would, therefore, be encouraged to make the statement: "I earned the privilege of staying up for an hour past my curfew on the weekend because I went to bed on time each day of the week."

   By framing such a statement in actual words, the child is mentally linking together his or her behavior in a cause and effect sequence. The more frequently that this occurs, the more likely it is that this will become a deeply embedded pattern of thinking. Ultimately, it is this kind of thinking that leads to the development of an internal locus of control.

9. Remember, parents and other adults set an example for children. Children learn by imitating those persons closest to them. If parents and other adults with whom the child associates have an internal locus of control, then it is far more likely that this will be transmitted to their children.

10. It takes time and effort to bring about a behavioral change, particularly if the child has developed bad habits. If we want children to be responsible, the goal can only be achieved in a step-by-step fashion. Children should begin with small responsibilities such as cleaning their room, taking out the trash, and so forth. This sets the foundation for coping with bigger responsibilities later on.

11. If the parents want their children to understand what is expected, they must be concrete in describing these expectations to them. Instead of saying "be nice" or "be good," parents should make statements such as, "Eat all of the vegetables on your plate," or "Be fully dressed for bed by 9:00 pm." Again, such clarity reduces the potential for misunderstandings, "power struggles," or other forms of resentment that might interfere with the processes of training the child to take responsibility for his or her actions.

In summary, it is important to keep in mind that what follows a behavior determines whether or not that behavior will continue. Rewards should always be given after the demonstration of responsibility, not before. Praising children for good behavior helps them to develop positive feelings about themselves. This sets the tone for the development of an internal locus of control. Moreover, instructing children in making actual statements connecting their actions with consequences can help bring this about as well. Rewarding and punishing a child must be done sensibly, fairly, and with the youngster's best interest in mind. This eliminates the likelihood that resentment, "power struggles," or other emotionally laden issues will interfere with the child's education and training. Further, it creates an environment that is much more conducive to learning and developing those positive attitudes upon which an internal locus of control is founded.

NOTES

1. Paul Lavin and Kathryn Lavin, *A Comprehensive Guide for Parenting the ADHD Child* (Baltimore, MD: Publish America, 2005), 23–32.

2. Paul Lavin, *Punishment Devolution: The "Missing Link" in Rearing Today's Children* (Baltimore, MD: Publish America, 2006), 19–28.

3. Paul Lavin, *Parenting the Overactive Child* (Lanham, MD: Madison Books, 1989), 22.

Chapter Twenty

An Internal Locus of Control Behavior Modification Program in the Home

The program that follows is designed to help the ADHD child to gain control of his or her behavior. Its purpose is to enable the youngster to learn to link his or her actions to their consequences. This cognitive connection, as discussed previously, is the foundation upon which the development of an internal locus of control is built. Moreover, it is the antidote for overcoming depression, which so frequently undermines the child's ability to put forth the necessary effort to cope with those everyday challenges of just being afflicted with ADHD. ADHD children who believe they can control what happens to them are far less likely to be encumbered by the sadness, hopelessness, and chronic demoralization, which plagues so many of their ADHD peers.

The proceeding behavior modification approach, by carefully programming rewards and penalties into the child's everyday schedule, teaches the youngster to make the mental connection between his or her actions and their immediate and long-term consequences. As noted earlier, if parents want children to act responsibly, they must follow these behaviors with pleasant consequences. By rewarding good planning and sustained effort, not only will the child's distractibility and impulsivity be addressed, but improved thinking and better behavior habits will be formed over time. In essence, a good behavior modification program will actually help to train ADHD children to make productive use of their high level of energy in such a way that an internal locus of control, the importance of which has been emphasized repeatedly, can become formed and integrated into their personality.

It should be noted that material rewards are used in this program to motivate the child to focus upon and complete work-oriented tasks. Material rewards are used because they are most likely to attract the child's interest and spur him or her into action. The youngster's desire to obtain such rewards serve as a motivating force to perform unpleasant tasks at home and school. Repeatedly completing these tasks, however, is what leads to the development of good work habits. Moreover, continued good performance makes it more likely that the child will acquire the feeling of satisfaction for a job well done. When these feelings of satisfaction occur repeatedly, the successful completion of work related tasks will then become its own reward. Hence, the motivation to initiate and sustain concentrated effort to achieve these goals will become internally rather than externally controlled. Thus, material rewards will no longer be necessary because the child will have learned to motivate him or herself from within.

One other point should be considered with regard to the following program. Although many parents, educators, and mental health professionals are familiar with behavior modification, this program is designed with a specific purpose in mind. The purpose is to train the ADHD child to not only engage in responsible behavior, but to sustain this over an extended period of time.[1,2] Thus, the program is geared to teach the youngster to organize and plan ahead on a daily, weekly, and even a monthly basis. The program actually trains the child to defer immediate gratification and to repeatedly exercise self-control and good judgment. For example, if the youngster does not plan ahead, he or she will not complete responsibilities within the appropriate time limits. This will result in the loss of special treats and privileges that most children would find to be desirable. On the other hand, if the youngster organizes and plans appropriately, valuable short and long-term rewards can be earned. Thus, through this approach, the child can learn that thinking ahead and the willingness to sustain concentrated effort can lead to the achievement of worthwhile goals.

With the preceding in mind, the next step is to specifically design the behavioral program. The program that will be presented is designed for children between ages of four or five to twelve years of age. In setting up the program, it is important to first decide the specific behaviors that the child is to perform each day. Next, the behaviors must be listed chronologically according to their order of occurrence with morning behaviors being first, afternoon behaviors being second, and evening behaviors being third. A sample of such behaviors and their chronological listing in Table 20.1.

In determining behaviors, it is important to list some tasks that the child is likely to complete relatively easily. This will enhance the likelihood that the ADHD youngster will receive some positive feedback right away for performing successfully and that he or she will become "hooked" into the system. Moreover, this will help to motivate the child to attempt the more difficult tasks that will also be required. Once the behaviors have been determined and arranged chronologically, they can be organized on a chart so that the youngster can follow them throughout the day.

Table 20.1.

Morning Behaviors	Afternoon Behaviors	Evening Behaviors
1. Be completely dressed by 7:30 a.m. 2. Wash hands and face. 3. Comb hair. 4. Eat all breakfast without complaining. 5. Brush teeth.	1. Eat all lunch without complaining. 2. Put clothes away. 3. Homework done neatly and accurately. 4. Put school materials in bookbag for next day. 5. Put toys away.	1. Eat supper without complaining. 2. Wash dishes. 3. Take bath. 4. Brush teeth. 5. Ready for bed by 8:30 p.m.

For children who cannot read, parents can draw pictures of the required activity or use pictures cut out from a magazine. These can serve as visual cues to remind the child to complete the task. Also, the chart can have a title such as Big Boy or Big Girl Chart. The title lets the child know that successful performance demonstrates responsibility and maturity. For older children, titles such as Maturity or Responsibility Chart might be used. A sample chart with the title and chronological listening of behaviors is shown in Table 20.2.

Once this has been completed, the next step is to identify inappropriate behaviors. These can be called Baby Behaviors because they show immaturity and a lack of responsibility. Again, such titles as Immature or Irresponsible Behaviors can be used with older children. These would appear in Table 20.3.

A list of inappropriate behaviors is included because it provides the child with feedback about actions that show poor self-control. However, it is important to emphasize the positive behaviors. These bring praise from parents, teachers, other adults, and even peers. It is praise and encouragement that ultimately motivates ADHD children and teaches them that they are capable of controlling themselves and performing successfully. And as noted earlier, this is the catalyst for helping the child to build an internal locus of control.

With the completion of the behavior chart, the next step is to develop a list of rewards that can be earned by successfully completing the assigned tasks. These rewards should be special treats that ordinarily could not be obtained during the course of the day, week or month. For example, special treats might include staying up an extra hour in the evening or ordering a special desert or snack. A special weekly treat requires that the child behave responsibly for a longer period of time. Thus, a bigger prize is offered such as going to a movie or a restaurant. A special super treat would require responsible behavior for two, three, or four weeks. Such treats might consist of a trip to an amusement park, both a movie and a restaurant, or earning an expensive toy. These separate lists on one chart enable the child to see what can be earned daily, weekly, and over the long-term. A sample completed reward chart would look like Table 20.4.

Table 20.2. Big Boy (or Girl) Chart.

	Sunday	Monday	Tuesday	Wednesday	Thursday	Friday	Saturday	Weekly Totals
Morning								
1. Dressed by 7:30 a.m.								
2. Properly groomed								
3. Eat breakfast without complaining								
Afternoon								
1. Homework done								
2. Take out trash								
3. Clean room								
Evening								
1. Eat supper without complaining								
2. Take bath								
3. Brush teeth								
4. Ready for bed by 8:30 p.m.								

Table 20.3.　Baby Behaviors

Baby Behaviors	Sun.	Mon.	Tues.	Wed.	Thurs.	Fri.	Sat.	Weekly Totals
1. Cursing								
2. Tantrum								
3. Lying								
4. Stealing								
5. Disobedience								
6. Back talk								

Tables 20.05 and 20.06 are completed samples of the Big Boy or Big Girl and Daily, Weekly, and Super Special Treats Charts that are ready to put into practice.

The reader will note that the behavior chart contains a percentage column. This portion tells the child how well he or she has done for the day and the week. The actual percentage determines whether the child will receive a reward. When

Table 20.4.

Daily Special Treats	Weekly Special Treats	Super Special Treats
1. 1 hr T.V. special	1. Fast food restaurant-limit $8	1. Amusement park (4 weeks-95%)
2. ½ hr extra staying up past bedtime	2. Movie	2. Camping (4 weeks-95%)
3. Special dessert	3. Skating	3. Restaurant of choice (4 weeks-90%)
4. Gum (1 piece)	4. Friend over for night	4. Trip to arcade-$15 limit (3 weeks-80%)
5. Soft drink	5 Friend for dinner	5. Fishing (3 weeks-80%)
6. Ice cream	6. Popcorn party	6. Baseball game (4 weeks-90%)
7. Chips	7. Order favorite meal at home	7. $20 toy (4 weeks-80%)
8. ½ hr. play game with parent	8. Stay up 2 hrs over bedtime-limit 1 night on weekend	8. $25 toy (4 weeks-90%)
9. Popcorn	9. $8 toy	9. Movie with friend, parent pay (3 weeks-90%)
10. Candy snack	10. Pizza	10. Bowling with friend, parent pay (3 weeks-90%)

Table 20.5. Big Boy (or Girl) Chart

	Sun	Mon	Tues	Wed	Thurs	Fri	Sat	Weekly Totals
Morning								
1. Dressed by 7:30 a.m.								
2. Eat breakfast w/o complaints								
3. Brush teeth								
Afternoon								
1. Homework done								
2. Pick up toys								
3. Feed dog								
Evening								
1. Eat supper w/o complains								
2. Wash dishes								
3. Take bath								
4. Ready for bed by 8:30 p.m.								
Baby Behaviors								
1. Complaining								
2. Tantrum								
3. Swearing								
4. Disobedience								
5. Taking things w/o permission								
6. Lying								
PERCENTAGES								

Table 20.6. Daily Special Treats, Weekly Special Treats, and Super Special Treats

Daily Special Treats	Weekly Special Treats	Super Special Treats
1. Chips	1. Movie	1. Baseball game (4 weeks-80%)
2. Soft drink	2. Bowling	2. Fishing (2 weeks-80%)
3. Ice cream	3. Friend overnight	3. Amusement Park (4 weeks-95%)
4. Stay up extra ½ hour	4. Go to friend overnight	4. $20 toy (3 weeks-90%)
5. Play Game with Parent ½ hr.	5. Pizza	5. DVD cartridge (4 weeks-90%)
6. Candy snack.	6. Fast food restaurant-$8 limit	6. Camping (3 weeks-90%)

the day is complete, the parents should compute the percentage and write it in the provided space. The child at this time can receive the reward. Depending on the availability of the reward, it may have to be delivered on the following day.

The reward system is based on the following guidelines. If the child completes 80% of the responsibilities with no baby behaviors, he or she would get to chose one item from the Daily Special Treats chart for that day. For 90% with no baby behaviors, two treats can be earned. For a perfect day, three treats can be obtained. If the youngster engages in a baby behavior, the successful performance of one responsibility is cancelled out. For example, let's suppose that the child was ready for school on time. However, he or she lied about something later on in the day. Lying would cancel out the credit that he or she would have received for being ready for school on time. Hence, the overall percentage for the day would be lowered.

The weekly special treats would be delivered in the same way as the daily specials. If the child successfully completed 80% of all possible responsible behaviors, he or she would choose one weekly special from the reward list. For 90%, two weekly specials could be obtained. For a perfect week, three specials could be earned. Keep in mind that the daily treats should be small prizes; whereas, the weekly prizes should be worth more. It is important to keep in mind that the rewards should be delivered as soon as the child has earned them if this is at all possible. Broken promises will not only discourage the child, but these will decrease the youngster's motivation to make the effort to perform successfully.

The Super Special Treats list differs from the daily and weekly specials because the delivery of these rewards requires more expense, time, and energy on the part of the parents. Since these rewards are more valuable, the child must behave responsibly for two, three, or four weeks in order to earn them. The purpose of this is to reward the child for working for extended periods of time in order to obtain more worthwhile goals. In order to earn these more valuable specials, the child must plan ahead. As noted earlier, training the child to think and plan ahead negates impulsivity and strengthens the child's ability to concentrate, complete assigned tasks, and gain greater self-control. This, in turn, makes it more likely that the child will become more confident and hopeful about his or her prospects for the future. It should be noted that on the Super Special Treats list, the time and percentage needed to earn the long-term rewards varies, depending on its overall value.

For example, the youngster would need an 80% performance for two weeks in order to go fishing. However, a trip to an amusement park, which might be more expensive and time consuming, requires a 95% performance for four weeks. By arranging the rewards on a two, three, and four week delivery basis with increasing percentages, parents are actually shaping the child to sustain good thinking, planning, and work habits over longer periods of time. This can help the child to learn that persistent effort can lead to achievement of more valuable goals in the future. Again, as with daily and weekly rewards, parents must be willing to invest the time, expense, and energy to ensure the delivery of Super Special Treats once they are earned. If such a treat is promised, we must be prepared to follow through if the program is to have credibility.

Once the chart is completed, the program is ready to put into practice. Each time a behavior is performed satisfactorily, a visible sign such as a gold star, a smiling face, or even a check is placed in the box beside the behavior for the day. Preferably, this should be done immediately after the task is completed. In the initial stages of the program, the ADHD child might need a reminder before performing an activity. However, more than one reminder is unacceptable. The failure to complete the task means that the box is left blank. Further, after a few weeks, no reminders should be given since parents want their child to function independently. It is important that nagging does not become the catalyst for bringing about good behavior. Rather, good behavior should come from within the child. This is indicative of the emergence and development of an internal locus of control, which as stressed throughout this book, is the antidote for overcoming depression.

One other point should be kept in mind. When a child satisfactorily completes a task, the parents should be prepared to acknowledge this. For example, parents might say to the child, "I like the way that you made your bed and cleaned your room" or "You did a good job washing the dishes." In other words, parents should tell the child that his or her behavior pleased them.

If the child behaves badly, negative feedback must also be provided. A visible sign such as a frowning face of a minus sign can be used. Again, specific feedback about the behavior must be provided. For example, the following might be stated: "When you dawdle while dressing in the morning, it causes you to be late for breakfast. Please dress more quickly the next time." Such a statement tells the child what he or she did that was wrong and why this behavior was harmful. Also, the statement provides the child with a better alternative. When parents reprimand, they may find that their child will react defensively to their criticism. If this occurs, arguing with the child is not likely to correct the problem. Rather, it would be better to remove the child from the situation until he or she is calm and ready to listen to their explanation. Distraught and oppositional children will not integrate that which is conveyed to them unless they are mentally and emotionally prepared to do so.

Another helpful suggestion in implementing the program is to have the ADHD child read the list of expected behaviors. Then have the youngster repeat the behaviors without looking at them. The child should be praised for each behavior that he or she remembers and reminded of those that are left out or forgotten. If the child cannot read, the parents should have him or her explain what is occurring in each of the pictures. They can then have the youngster explain the behaviors without looking at them. Remember, asking the ADHD child to verbally repeat the behaviors makes it more likely that he or she will retain them and behave appropriately.

Another strategy is also useful in teaching the ADHD child to think ahead and to avoid the temptation of evading responsibility. The youngster and the parents can select special shows from a schedule of TV programs that the child would like to see when his or her work is completed. Further, the youngster might pick out some of the weekly and super special treats that he or she would like to earn. This approach teaches the child to think ahead so that these goals can be achieved more readily.

An example of a fully completed weekly chart and an interpretation of how this would be used can be seen in Table 20.7.

Note that on the first day (Sunday), the child scored 100%. Therefore, he would get to choose three daily special treats from the reward chart presented in Table 20.8.

On Monday, although the youngster completed nine of the ten tasks satisfactorily, one bad behavior occurred. This dropped the daily percentage to 80 instead of 90 percent because the frowning face cancelled out one of the smiling faces. As a result, only one special treat could be obtained for that day. On Thursday, the child completed all of the tasks successfully. However, two violations occurred, thereby dropping the daily percentage from 100 to 80 percent. As a result, only one, rather than three rewards, could be chosen from the Daily Special Treats chart. On Saturday, nine of the tasks were satisfactorily completed, but three violations occurred. Thus, three of the successfully

Table 20.7. Big Boy (or Girl) Chart

	Sun	Mon	Tues	Wed	Thurs	Fri	Sat	Weekly Totals
Morning 1. Ready for school by 7:30a.m.	☺		☺	☺	☺	☺	☺	6/7 86%
2. Eat breakfast w/o complaining	☺	☺	☺	☺	☺	☺	☺	7/7 100%
3. Brush teeth	☺	☺	☺	☺	☺	☺	☺	7/7 100%
Afternoon 1. Complete homework	☺	☺	☺	☺	☺	☺	☺	7/7 100%
2. Put toys away	☺	☺	☺	☺	☺	☺	☺	7/7 100%
3. Take out trash	☺	☺	☺	☺	☺	☺	☺	7/7 100%
Evening 1. Set table	☺	☺	☺	☺	☺	☺		6/7 86%
2. Take bath	☺	☺	☺	☺	☺	☺	☺	7/7 100%
3. Brush teeth	☺	☺	☺	☺	☺	☺	☺	7/7 100%
4. Ready for bed by 8:30 p.m.	☺	☺	☺	☺	☺	☺	☺	7/7 100%
Baby Behaviors 1. Complaining		☹					☹	2
2. Tantrum					☹		☹	2
3. Swearing					☹			1
4. Disobedience			☹					1
5. Taking things w/o permission								
6. Lying							☹	1
PERCENTAGES	100%	80%	90%	100%	80%	100%	70%	89%

Table 20.8. Daily Special Treats

1. Candy Snack
2. 1 hr. TV special
3. ½ hr. extra on bedtime
4. Special dessert
5. Pizza slice
6. 1 piece gum
7. Soft drink
8. Ice cream
9. Chips or popcorn
10. Play game with parents ½ hour

Table 20.9.   Weekly Special Treats

1. Trip to fast food restaurant-$8 limit
2. Movie
3. Skating
4. Friend overnight
5. Friend for lunch
6. Stay overnight w/ friend
7. $8 toy
8. Popcorn party w/ friend
9. Order favorite meal at home
10. Stay up 1½ hours beyond bedtime on weekend

completed tasks were cancelled out. Since the child's daily percentage was only 70, no daily rewards could be obtained.

The reader will note that the weekly as well as the daily percentages are given for each task. Also, a total percentage for the week is provided, which in this case was 89%. Thus, the child can obtain one weekly special treat from the reward chart in Table 20.9.

Although this case example covers only through the Weekly Special Treats chart, the same principles that were previously discussed would be applied in obtaining super special treats. The only difference is that the child would have to behave responsibly for longer periods of time. Note that on the Super Special Treats chart (Table 20.10), a time period and percentage for successfully completed tasks is presented. This enables the youngster to know in advance what is required to obtain the reward.

During the administration of this program, it is helpful to have a family meeting for approximately ten to fifteen minutes each evening. At this time, parents and children can talk about successfully and unsuccessfully completed tasks and the implementation of strategies that might be used to im-

Table 20.10.   Super Special Treats

1. Restaurant (2 weeks-90%)
2. Amusement park (4 weeks-95%)
3. Camping (3 weeks-95%)
4. Fishing (4 weeks-90%)
5. Baseball game (4 weeks-90%)
6. $25 toy (4 weeks-90%)
7. Movie with friend, parents pay (3 weeks-90%)
8. Arcade $10 limit (2 weeks-80%)
9. Fast food restaurant with friend $10 limit (2 weeks-90%)
10. Trip to zoo (3 weeks-80%)

prove upon or to maintain a good performance. At the end of the meeting, parents should ask the youngster to identify those behaviors that were performed successfully as well as those that need to be improved upon the next day. If the child can accurately identify and talk about the preceding, he or she should be praised accordingly. If the child forgets some points, the parents should help him or her to recall what was discussed.

By using this approach, the parents will be training their child to concentrate, to plan ahead, and to build a strong track record of performing successfully. As stressed many time, this is the foundation upon which an internal locus of control and an optimistic attitude are built. And this is the "medicine" that is needed for curing the demoralization and hopelessness that so frequently undermines the ADHD child's willingness to make the necessary effort to succeed.

As indicated previously, the preceding program will be effective with children from approximately four or five to twelve years of age. In order to work with youngsters from two to four years of age, a more simplified version is needed.[3] In light of this, the following suggestions are offered. With two or four year olds, parents should explain and demonstrate the appropriate behaviors. Moreover, they should have the child actually perform them as well. When the child engages in a "big boy" or "big girl" behavior, praise should be given immediately along with some tangible reward.

For example, the child might receive a poker chip each time he or she behaves appropriately. These can then be placed in a jar where the child can see them accumulate. Once a certain number of chips have been acquired, they can be redeemed for a special treat such as a candy bar, a snack, or some other trinket or small reward. More valuable long-term rewards such as a trip to purchase a toy would cost a greater number of chips. These could only be gained by saving chips instead of spending them on short-term rewards. Teaching the youngster to count and to associate a certain number of chips with the purchasing of a reward can train him or her to concentrate, to think before acting (the antidote to impulsivity), and to make the cognitive connection between his or her behavior and its consequences. Again, these are the beginning of building an internal locus of control within the mental structure of young children. And it is during these early and most formative years that such traits start to develop and become an integral part of the youngster's personality formation.

Another technique, which can be particularly effective with young children, is to take a picture of a toy and cut it into several pieces. The individual parts can then be put together like a puzzle. Each time the youngster behaves appropriately, one of the parts can be assembled. If the child behaves poorly, one or more pieces can be taken away or the child may be required to start over again. When the entire puzzle is completed, the youngster can go with the parents to purchase the toy. Again, such an approach facilitates the development of good thinking and work habits, which are the foundation for the formation of an internal locus of control.

Another very simple approach that can be used with small children is to buy a variety of cartoon and animal stickers and gold stars. Take a large piece of paper, and in large bold print, put BIG BOY or BIG GIRL on the top. Each time that the child behaves appropriately, he can choose a sticker or star and paste it on the paper. A special sticker that the child might like can be awarded when a particularly difficult task requiring extra self-control is mastered. For instance, when the child is successful in tying his or her shoes, a special sticker might be provided.

In conclusion, in working with children between the ages of two and four, it is important that parents have the child both verbally describe and demonstrate what is expected. Further, it is important to praise the child and provide immediate feedback when the youngster behaves properly. This shows that parents are interested in how the child acts. By reinforcing appropriate behavior, parents are helping the youngster to develop a positive outlook on life during his or her most fledgling years. This, as noted numerous times, is the foundation upon which an internal locus of control is built.

One final point should be stressed. The use of material rewards and charts is a simple technique to motivate the child to plan ahead, to make good choices, and to persist in the achievement of worthwhile goals. This approach is utilized because it provides the ADHD child with the structure and incentive to want to perform successfully. As the child learns to organize his or her time properly and develops good work habits, these external cues and motivators will be less necessary. At this point, the pursuit of excellence and the satisfaction of a job well done become their own reward. It is this attitude that parents want to foster in their child. Behavior modification is simply one of the tools that can be put into practice to help them to achieve this goal.

NOTES

1. Paul Lavin, *Parenting the Overactive Child* (Lanham, MD: Madison Books, 1989), 27–42.

2. Paul Lavin and Kathryn Lavin, *A Comprehensive Guide for Parenting the ADHD Child* (Baltimore, MD: Publish America), 33–45.

3. Paul Lavin and Kathryn Lavin, *A Comprehensive Guide*, 47–49.

Chapter Twenty-One

A Locus of Control Behavior Modification Program in the School

No book on the ADHD child would be complete without a chapter on applying behavior modification principles in the school. Beginning at the age four or five, many children spend approximately six hours a day at the school. During this time, the youngster is faced with a number of intellectual, social, and emotional challenges. Successful performance of these tasks is important if the child is to develop an internal locus of control and the self-confidence associated with this. Youngsters who do poorly throughout their school years and go on to become successful adults are the exception, rather than the rule. Many children who fall behind in reading, writing, and mathematics do not simply catch up with the passage of time. Without extra help and tutoring, they usually fall further and further behind. Also, these young people tend to develop an external locus of control, frequently blaming the school, the teachers, and other children for their learning and social problems. Moreover, the child's dissatisfaction with school spills over into the home, leading to resistance, arguing, and acting-out when parents try to address this problem or to hold the child accountable for completing homework assignments. If the youngster is unhappy at school, the chances are that he or she will be unhappy at home as well. What happens at school, therefore, can not be ignored. Parents and teachers must work together should problems arise.

In my work with parents, I have never met a parent who failed to recognize the importance of a good education. However, I have met many discouraged parents who did not know how to motivate their children to study in preparation for the future. They, like their ADHD children, often appeared to be frustrated, depressed, and demoralized nearly to the point of hopelessness. It was obvious that these parents needed help from the school in order to reverse the downward spiral that appeared to consistently plague them and their seemingly forever, errant child.

The following suggestions for arranging the educational environment to achieve this goal should be considered.[1,2] The school, if it is to be helpful, must provide the parents with consistent feedback on the ADHD child's performance so that they can reinforce that which is being learned in the classroom. Again, it must be kept in mind that the motivation of the ADHD child (or almost any child for that matter) is determined by what follows the youngster's behavior. If pleasant consequences follow a behavior, it is more likely to continue. If negative consequences follow, the behavior is more likely to terminate. These are very simple but basic laws that serve as a guideline for understanding almost all human behavior. If it makes sense to use this approach at home, then it would be reasonable to expect that it should be applied in school as well. The key, however, is to make sure that it is implemented properly.

In working with teachers, I have occasionally encountered skeptics who have been unsuccessful in using behavior modification with a stubborn ADHD child. They contended, "I have tried everything and nothing works." Further inquiry, however, usually showed that behavior modification was not at fault for the failure. Rather, poor management, the improper use of punishment, inconsistency, or the failure to provide appropriate rewards were responsible for the program's shortcomings. If we want to motivate ADHD children, the proper and consistent application of behavioral principles must be applied. First, those behaviors that are prerequisites to learning should be clearly identified and rewarded accordingly. Second, those behaviors that detract or interfere with the child's learning must also be specified and either ignored (if this is possible) or immediately penalized.

In light of the preceding, it would make sense, therefore, that the teacher's initial task would be to identify those behaviors that enhance and detract from the ADHD student's performance in the classroom environment. Following this, these should be clearly communicated to the child. For example, specific instructions such as, "Sit upright in your chair with your feet flat on the floor and face the front of the classroom" or "Put your reading book, pencil, paper, and eraser on your desk" are much more exact than statements such as, "Be good" or "Please act more maturely." The latter instructions are often unclear and confusing, particularly with younger children. The former, however, identify specific behaviors that are more likely to facilitate learning in the classroom. Other sample behaviors that are often prerequisites to learning in the classroom are as follows:

1. Focus your eyes directly on the teacher or the assigned task.
2. Have the proper materials (identify these) on the desk for each lesson.
3. Complete the work neatly, accurately, and according to the instructions.
4. Complete homework neatly, accurately, and according to the instructions.
5. Enter and leave the room silently (without talking).
6. Raise your hand before speaking; talk only when given permission.
7. Begin assignment immediately.
8. Ask questions only when you don't understand an assignment.
9. Listen and follow directions the first time.
10. Put all books and materials inside your desk.

These are just some of the behaviors that might be required if the ADHD child is to be helped in attending to the task at hand. It is important to keep in mind that learning demands concentration. If a youngster has slovenly work habits and spends time fidgeting or looking around the classroom, it is highly unlikely that he or she will be a successful student. Further, if a child interrupts or is noisy and disruptive, this interferes with other students' ability to concentrate and learn as well. Thus, there are certain behaviors in which the child must engage if he or she is to get the most out of the classroom environment. Parents and teachers must be certain that the ADHD youngster is performing these in a satisfactory manner. This helps the child to use his or her abilities to the fullest and enhances the youngster's prospects for a better future.

As noted previously, it is important to encourage and reward proper behavior in the classroom if we want to help the child to develop an internal locus of control. The classroom teacher then should have a plan for reinforcing those children who behave as expected. Moreover, if a student fails to fulfill his or her responsibilities, a penalty should be applied as well. Some sample rewards for reinforcing appropriate classroom behavior are as follows:

1. Reading a book or magazine
2. Free time on the classroom computer
3. Performing responsibilities (e.g. passing out paper, collecting materials, helping the teacher).
4. Carrying a message to the office.
5. Being first in line.
6. Using art materials
7. Sending home a "good boy" or "good girl" note for the day.
8. Sending home a certificate verifying responsible behavior for that day. An example is in Figure 21.1.

```
┌─────────────────────────────────────────────────────────────┐
│                    RESPONSIBLE BEHAVIOR                        │
│                      CERTIFICATE TO                            │
│   Name: _____                       │
│   Date:_____                       │
│                                                               │
└─────────────────────────────────────────────────────────────┘
```

Figure 21.1.   Responsible Behavior Certificate.

9. Gold stars or stickers of various types.
10. A movie for the class.
11. No homework for the evening.
12. Extra recess or play time.
13. Listening to music or a story.
14. Statements of approval or praise, particularly in the presence of peers or other adult authority.
15. Invite and eat lunch with a friend.
16. Recognition for being "student of the day" or "student of the week."
17. Appointment to a leadership position.
18. Appointment to the "safety patrol."
19. Extra play time for the class.
20. Each lunch with the teacher.
21. Call or email parents on good behavior.
22. Students call parents on school phone to report good behavior.
23. Work on an arts and crafts project of choice.
24. Inexpensive small trinkets, gadgets, and trading cards.
25. Trip to the principal's office with teacher to report good behavior and have lunch with the principal.

Another type of reward system that works with young children involves giving the youngster a small piece of paper with a smiling face on it each time that he or she is "caught" behaving appropriately. A word of praise in large bold capital letters is printed on top of the paper, and a space to insert the child's name is on the bottom under the smiling face. Samples of these are in Figure 21.2.

When the child receives one of the above, he or she can write his or her name in the space provided. They can then deposit the paper into a large jar. At the end of the week, the teacher might conduct a raffle in which three or more names might be drawn. Each winner would receive a small prize. Naturally, the more good behavior papers the child receives, the more chances that he or she would have for winning a prize.

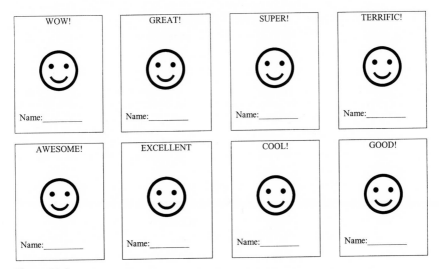

Figure 21.2.

As an aside, this technique also works well for parents who want their children to behave appropriately when the family takes a trip together. Each time that the child shows good self-control, one of the good behavior papers can be awarded. These could each be cashed in during the trip for a nickel, a dime, or a quarter. The accumulated sum could be spent at an amusement park or some other place that children enjoy.

In addition to rewards for good behavior, penalties for poor behavior must also be applied.[3] Some sample punishments that might be used are as follows:

1. Isolation from the class
2. Poor grades
3. Sending the child to the office
4. Calling the parents
5. Having the child call the parents and report his or her misbehavior.
6. A note to the parents that has to be signed and returned
7. The child writes a note to the parents reporting his or her poor conduct.
8. Loss of recess time.
9. Take home and finish incomplete work during recreation time.
10. Write 100 sentences stating the proper behavior to be engaged in.
11. A verbal reprimand from the administrative staff.
12. Detention

For teachers and parents, who are interested in a variety of other penalties that can be successfully applied in altering in and out-of-school behavior, this author's book entitled *Punishment Devolution: The "Missing Link" in Rearing Today's Children* is recommended. This book focuses upon the proper application of punishment and specific guidelines and techniques for putting this into practice. Unfortunately, in today's child-rearing climate, the importance of punishment is often overlooked or given cursory consideration in the practice of behavior modification. This needs to be corrected so that a proper balance utilizing both rewards and penalties can be effectively instituted and appropriately applied.

It is important for parents to get consistent feedback from the school so that they can reward and penalize the child accordingly at home. This will support what the classroom teacher is attempting to achieve with the child. Consistent and specific feedback not only reinforces what the school is attempting to accomplish, but it makes it more likely that this will help the youngster to develop those skills necessary for successful performance. It is of the utmost importance for the school to provide parents with daily feedback on the child's behavior if this is at all possible. A note at the end of the week or every few weeks is not satisfactory. Too much time passes between the time that parents receive the feedback and the actual occurrence of the child's behavior. It must be kept in mind that if we want to increase or decrease certain behaviors, rewards and penalties must follow these as closely as possible. Holding the child accountable every day makes it more likely that he or she will acquire good work habits, leading to the development of an internal locus of control. Once these have been developed and maintained for a period of time, then feedback from the school every few weeks would be appropriate. A daily check list that the teacher might use to provide such feedback shown in Table 21.1.

It should only take the teacher a few seconds to fill out the checklist for each class. Little extra work is required on the teacher's part. However, par-

Table.21.1.   Behaviors

Behaviors	Class	Class	Class	Class	Class
1. Begins work promptly	Yes_____ No_____	Yes_____ No_____	Yes_____ No_____	Yes_____ No_____	Yes_____ No_____
2. Has proper materials	Yes_____ No_____	Yes_____ No_____	Yes_____ No_____	Yes_____ No_____	Yes_____ No_____
3. Completes class work neatly & accurately	Yes_____ No_____	Yes_____ No_____	Yes_____ No_____	Yes_____ No_____	Yes_____ No_____
4. Completes homework satisfactorily	Yes_____ No_____	Yes_____ No_____	Yes_____ No_____	Yes_____ No_____	Yes_____ No_____
5. Conduct rating for the day	Good_____ Fair_____ Poor_____	Good_____ Fair_____ Poor_____	Good_____ Fair_____ Poor_____	Good_____ Fair_____ Poor_____	Good_____ Fair_____ Poor_____
6. Teacher signature					

ents will still obtain a considerable amount of information on their child's daily performances. The teacher simply has to check Yes or No and rate the child's conduct for the day. If in a specific class (e.g. music or art) a particular category (e.g. completes homework satisfactorily) does not apply, the teacher can put a large X through that box. The X will indicate that this particular category does not count in the assessment of the child's overall performance for the day. For instance, in the Music class a homework assignment may not be given by the teacher. Thus, a large X would be placed in this Yes or No box. This would eliminate that box from the tabulation of the child's overall performance score. In using the check list with pre-school and first grade youngsters, smiling or frowning faces can be put into the boxes in place of Yes or No. Finally, the teacher's signature would be required for each class to verify the accuracy of the information that is provided. If the signature is missing, then the score for each of the categories (whether these are filled in or not) automatically becomes zero. Moreover, each zero category would be tabulated into the total of possible points that could have been earned for that day. It is important, therefore, that the child makes sure that the teacher signs the sheet accordingly for each of the attended classes.

Once the program has been put into effect, parents can begin to reward and penalize their child for his and her performance at school. It is important to stress to the youngster that the check list must come home. It must not become misplaced or lost because the child has a bad day. If parents are using the home based behavior modification program described previously, one of the ways to earn a check or a smiling face would be bring the check list home regardless of whether it was good or bad. This reinforces honesty and makes it more likely that the check list will come home each day. The failure to arrive with the check list, however, should result in a frowning face or a minus sign going into the IRRESPONSIBILITY or BABY BEHAVIORS column. Further, it might also result in a loss of play or TV privileges for that day. Thus, it would make sense for the youngster to make sure that the check list comes home.

The next step is to devise a system for rewarding a good day at school. First, each Yes that the child receives would be one point. A Good in conduct would be two points; a Fair would be one point; and a No or Poor would receive zero points. In the sample sheet, the child could earn a total of 30 points for the day (one point for each Yes and two points for each Good for each class); 6 points per class multiplied by 5 classes equals 30 points per day. The 30 point total would be less if X marks are inserted into a box because it does not apply for that class.

We might then decide that 80% of the total possible points would be considered a good day (24 points for example); 90% (27 points) would be an excellent day; and 100% (30 points) would be a super day. Anything less than 80%, however, would mean that the child had a bad day, which would not be rewarded. For a score of 80%, the youngster would earn one small reward. For 90%, two small rewards would be earned. A perfect check list (100%) would earn three small rewards. Also, a weekly, bi-weekly, tri-weekly, and monthly reward schedule for 80, 90, or 95% of the possible total points might be devised as indicated previously. This will encourage the child to maintain a solid performance over an extended period of time. As noted earlier, this will help to firmly establish good work habits.

Another technique which would be helpful with older ADHD children who are behaving poorly is the use of a contingency contract. In this approach, a written agreement is made between parents and the child. The parents promise to deliver a reward if the youngster scores 80, 90, or 100% of the possible points on the check list. A sample contingency contract appears in Figure 21.3.

Note that in this sample a weekly format is used. However, the contract dates could be for a daily, weekly, bi-weekly, tri-weekly, or monthly period. Again, the 80, 90, and 100% rewards can be determined from the material that was previously presented. This could then be written into the contract. Also, a penalty clause could be added in order to punish irresponsible behav-

---

BEHAVIOR CONTRACT

Contract dates: _____ to _____
                    (beginning date)   (termination date)

Contractual parties _____   _____
                         (parent)   (child)

I _____ agree to the following in order to improve my performance at school.
        (child)

If I score 80 percent on my school check list then my parents will

_____
                              (reward)

If I score 90 percent on my school check list then my parents will

_____
                              (reward)

If I score 100 percent on my school check list then my parents will

_____
                              (reward)

                              Signatures

                    _____   _____
                      (parent)   (parent)

                         _____
                           (child)

                         _____
                          (teacher)

Figure 21.3.   Behavior Contract.

ior. For example, if the child "forgets" to bring home the check list or scores less than 80% for the week, penalties could be applied such as the loss of play or TV privileges or "grounding" for the day or weekend.

All contracts should be typed so that they look "official." This helps to let the child know that the agreement is a serious matter and not something to be taken lightly. When the contract is completed, all involved persons should sign their names in the appropriate places. A copy should be given to all participants, including the child. This will enable him or her to refer to the terms of this agreement if necessary. Providing the child with a copy eliminates the use of excuses such as "You didn't say that" or "I forgot." It is important to note that there is a space for the teacher's name on the contract. The teacher's signature along with that of the parents shows that the home and the school are working together. The child, therefore, will be unable "to play one off against the other."

In summary, it is important for parents to attend to their ADHD child's educational progress in the school. This is where the youngster learns those academic and social skills that lead to successful achievement and the development of an internal locus of control. Those children who work diligently at school will be better prepared to face life's challenges. Parents are not necessarily experts in educational psychology. However, they can become quite knowledgeable about what it takes to motivate their child and those psychodynamic factors that influence their particular youngster's behavior. Being equipped with such knowledge will help parents to determine whether the classroom environment is organized in a manner that facilitates academic learning and the development of responsible behaviors. If the teacher has clearly defined expectations on how students should behave in class and these behaviors are rewarded and penalized accordingly, the child should prosper.

It is important to keep in mind that if parents want ADHD children to behave responsibly, they must reward this on a consistent basis. This enables positive work habits to be formed and maintained. Such habits do not develop with the simple passage of time or by chance. Rather, sensible planning and cooperation between the home and school are needed in order to bring this about. If there are indications that the child is not performing as expected, particularly in the early years, it is important that daily school feedback be provided. This enables the parents to reinforce what the school is doing by rewarding and penalizing the child at home. Holding the child accountable makes it more likely that the youngster will develop the kind of work habits leading to success. And accountability can be best achieved by using a daily check list and requiring that the youngster bring this home. In order to establish good work habits, feedback on the child's performance at school cannot wait two, three, or four weeks. Too much time elapses between the time that the behavior occurs and the application of the consequences. However, once a consistently positive behavior pattern is established, then a weekly, bi-weekly, or monthly feedback system may be enough to maintain the child's gains.

One final point is worthy of note. Parents might find the teacher to be resistant to the use of behavioral approaches despite the fact that the child is not performing as expected. If this occurs, parents should seek out the advice and service of the school counselor or psychologist. If these professionals are too over-burdened to respond quickly, parents should consider obtaining the services of a qualified private child psychologist. He or she could work with the school on the child's behalf. It is hoped that such assistance will not be needed. However, parents should be aware of and prepared to use all available options. The child's education is a most important priority.

Finally, it is essential to again emphasize that parents and teachers must work together to train ADHD youngsters in the acquisition of good work habits. If both parties use sensible principles to guide and shape the child's behavior, it is far more likely that the youngster will perform successfully. This then will lead to the development of an internal locus of control, which is the antidote to depression, and the formation of a more positive self-concept.

NOTES

1. Paul Lavin, *Parenting the Overactive child* (Lanham, MD: Madison Books, 1989), 93–103.

2. Paul Lavin and Kathryn Lavin, *A Comprehensive Guide for Parenting the ADHD Child* (Baltimore, MD: Publish America, 2005), 51–61.

3. Paul Lavin, *Punishment Devolution: The "Missing Link in Rearing Today's Children* (Baltimore, MD: Publish America, 2006), 94–105.

Chapter Twenty-Two

Summary and Conclusions

As the preceding emphasizes, chronic depression can be an emotional "killer," which can seriously undermine the effective treatment of ADHD children. Depression, superimposed on or co-existing with ADHD, is not an uncommon problem. As noted earlier, up to 30% of ADHD children are diagnosed as being clinically depressed. And this does not take into account those youngsters who are chronically sad or "down in the dumps" most of the time. The latter may have escaped the clinician's label. However, these unfortunate youngsters, like their formally diagnosed ADHD peers, have little hope that their efforts will improve the quality of their lives.

The failure to successfully treat ADHD can lead to more serious behavioral disorders later on. For instance, it is not unusual for ADHD children to become oppositional defiant (Oppositional Defiant Disorder) and antisocial (Conduct Disorder) as they pass through the developmental spectrum. The more serious disturbances are founded upon the negative behavioral and emotional turmoil that remained untreated during the child's most formative years. It is these unidentified emotional issues that are the catalyst leading to more serious problems, which emerge during the adolescent and adult years. Interestingly, the data indicate that over 40% of adults diagnosed with ADHD suffer from depression. This higher number, in comparison with those figures on depression with ADHD children, would suggest that depression is overlooked in the earlier years and, if left untreated, actually increases with the passage of time.[1]

The first step that must be taken in treating the ADHD child's depression is to understand and acknowledge its existence. If we sincerely attempt to "walk in the ADHD child's shoes," it is easy to see why he or she might feel demoralized much of the time. Moreover, it is easy to understand why the child fails to make the necessary effort to cope with his or her difficulties. Why try when you have little or no confidence that you efforts will succeed? For a morose, despondent child, it is much easier to withdraw, act out, and blame others for his or her problems. In fact, ADHD children who engage in the latter are more likely to have a very poor self-concept. Because they lack confidence, ADHD children are quick to argue and make excuses even when helpful and sincere criticism is presented to them. From their point of view any form of criticism, even that which could be beneficial, is like rubbing salt into an open wound. With such a mental set, all corrective instruction whether it be positive or negative, is lumped into a single, derogatory "you are putting me down" category. This type of single minded, compartmentalized thinking then leads to the excuse making, acting out, and blaming, which was referred to earlier. Such a defensive mode prevents the emotionally charged youngster from taking in and processing valuable information, which is communicated to him or her. As a result, he or she is likely to repeat the same mistakes again and again. Hence, this defensive barrier, which interferes with the child's ability to learn, must be brought down if more productive thinking and behavioral changes are to occur.

The antidote for combating depression is helping the ADHD youngster to develop an internal locus of control. As emphasized previously, this entails teaching the child to make a mental connection between his or her behavior and its consequences. The youngster, who is able to accurately make this connection, not only has the potential for acquiring greater self-control, but he will be much better equipped to anticipate the consequences of his actions and to make better plans for achieving success in the future. And the achieving of success, particularly for an emotionally starved ADHD child, can be an exhilarating experience. It can produce a positive "up beat" emotional state, leading to an increased willingness to try when challenges arise. This new mental set ("It is my behavior that is responsible for what happens. If I make the effort, I can succeed."), then becomes the catalyst for replacing depression and defensiveness with optimism and true self-confidence.

Teaching the ADHD child to develop an internal locus of control is a multifaceted task. Setting up a highly structured behavior modification program and coordinating this between the home and school may be necessary. A properly designed and implemented behavior modification program specifically teaches the child that his or her behavior leads to pleasant or unpleasant consequences. Such an approach, in combination with a plan for teaching the child to think constructively and to accurately label and to alter his or her emotional state, completes this training package.

It is important to keep in mind that ADHD children may harbor old resentments based on how they have been treated in the past. Rumination and preoccupation with such unresolved emotional issues can sabotage even the best conceived psychological and educational plans. Deep seated frustration, anger, hurt, and feelings of hopelessness founded on the youngster's perception of being treated unfairly or in a mean fashion can be a major road block to altering the child's cognitive and emotional state. This is why these overlooked and unresolved issues must be rooted out and dealt with accordingly. Again, the failure to do this undermines our best and most sincere efforts to help the struggling and resistant ADHD child.

Unlike many books on treating ADHD children, this text focuses on depression and how this interferes with the youngster's ability to learn and to cope with his or her inattentiveness and impulsivity. It is during the early years, when the child's personality is most malleable, that this needs to be addressed. Negative thinking and feeling, and counterproductive behavioral patterns, if not dealt with in the fledgling years, can become deeply embedded personality traits. These can then become increasingly more difficult to alter with the passage of time.

All children begin life's journey wanting to achieve successfully and to win the respect of their parents, teachers, and peers. ADHD children are no different in this regard. However, because they are prone to become easily distracted and to act impulsively, they begin early in life to be chastised for their failure to exhibit better self-control. Like most youngsters, such negative feedback can leave gaping unhealed emotional wounds. If not nurtured and attended to, these can cause the child to develop a cavalier and belligerent "I don't care" approach to life. However, the manifestation of such behavior is simply a veneer. It is only a cover for an emotional malaise, which is the real fuel powering the child's sputtering and lurching behavioral engine.

Being sensitive to this is not easy for most of us. This occurs because the ADHD child, who makes little noticeable effort to change, can grate on our nerves. This can cause us to react insensitively and harshly, especially when we have made sincere attempts to be helpful. The key to curbing our own reactions is to recognize that it is depression and the self-degradation associated with this that is largely responsible for the child's actions. Unlike adults, ADHD children lack the experience and insight that comes with age. Most importantly, however, they lack skill in the understanding of words and language and how these can be used to make conscious alterations in their thinking, emotions, and behavior.

As parents, educators, and mental health professionals, it is up to us to help them to acquire these skills. It is our willingness to put the principles outlined in this book into actual practice that will enable depressed ADHD children to become better participants in coping with their own problems. Helping these youngsters to replace demoralization with hopefulness is the key ingredient to achieving this goal. This, in essence, is the catalyst for motivating these youngsters to invest the necessary effort to achieve successfully both now and in the future.

NOTE

1. Lynn Weiss, *Attention Deficit Disorder in Adults* (Lanham, MD: Taylor Trade Publishing, 2005), 53–65.

Bibliography

American Psychological Association. *Quick Reference To the Diagnostic Criteria From DSM-IV.* Washington, DC: American Psychiatric Association, 1994.

Anxiety and Depression Solutions. "Common Disorders Associated with ADHD." http://www.anxiety-and-depressionsoluation.com/articles/adhddisorder010305 .htm (26, January, 2006).

Bernstein, Jeffrey. "When ADHD Combines with Depression." *Depression Can Often Co-Exist with AD/HD.* 2003. http://www.drjeffonline.com/low/?d=1642152.0374 (26, January 2006).

Ellis, Albert, "Emotional Disturbance and its Treatment In a Nutshell." *Canadian Counselor 5, no.3* (1974): 168–171.

Erickson, Erik. *Childhood and Society.* New York: Norton, 1963.

Francois, Guy R. *The Lifespan.* Belmont, CA: Wadsworth Publishing, 1999.

Goldstein, Sam, and Michael Goldstein. *Managing Attention Disorders in Children.* New York: John Wiley & Sons, 1990.

Hallowel, Edward, and John Ritey. *Delivered From Distraction: Getting the most out of life with Attention Deficit Disorder.* New York: Touchstone, 1994.

Hartman, Thom. Edison *Gene: ADHD and the Gift of the Hunter Child.* Rochester, VT: Park Street Press, 2003.

Havighurst, Robert, J. *Developmental Tasks and Education.* New York: D. McKay, 1979.

Honos-Webb, Laura. *The Gift of ADHD.* Oakland, CA: New Harbinger Publications, 2004.

Jensen, Peter. "Attention-Deficit/Hyperactivity Disorder." *About Mental Illness.* 2003. http://www.nami.org/Templatecf.../TagedPageDisplay.cfm8TPLID=54Content ID=2304 (26, January, 2006).

Kohlberg, Lawrence A. *The Meaning and Measurement of Moral Development.* Worcester, MA: Clark University Press, 1980.

Lavin, Paul, and Cynthia Park. *Despair Turned Into Rage.* Washington, DC: CWLA Press, 1999.

Lavin, Paul, and Kathryn Lavin. *A Comprehensive Guide for Parenting the ADHD Child*. Baltimore, MD: Publish American, 2005.

Lavin, Paul, and Kathryn Lavin. *Koping for Kids: A Coping Skills Program for Elementary School Children*. Minneapolis, MN: Educational Media Corp., 2005.

Lavin, Paul. "Cognitive Restructuring: A Counseling Approach for Improving the ADHD Child's Self-Concept." *Dimensions of Counseling* 30, no.2 (August, 2002): 22–27.

Lavin, Paul. *Parenting the Overactive Child*. Lanham, MD: Madison Books, 1989.

Lavin, Paul. *Profiles in Fury*. East Rockaway, New York: Cummings & Hathaway, 1998.

Lavin, Paul. *Punishment Devolution: The "Missing Link" in Rearing Today's Children*. Baltimore, MD: Publish America, 2006.

Lavin, Paul. *Teaching Kids to Think Straight*. Columbia, MO: Hawthorne Educational Services, 1991.

Lavin, Paul. *Working With Angry and Violent Youth*. Columbia, MO: Hawthorne Educational Services, 1996.

Lazarus, Arnold, and Allen Fay. *I Can If I Want To*. New York: Warner Books, 1977.

Lewis, Marilyn. "The Upside of ADHD." *MSN Health & Fitness*. 2006. http: health.msn.com/centers/adhd/article page.aspx?cp-documentid=100109339 (6, April 2006).

Mish, Frederick C., ed. *Webster's Ninth New Collegiate Dictionary*. Springfield, MA: Merriam-Webster, 1984.

Patterson, C.H. *Theories of Counseling and Psychotherapy*. New York: Harper & Row, 1973.

Polivy, Janet, and Peter C. Herman. "If At First You Don't Succeed: False Hope of Self-Change." *American Psychologist* 57, no.9 (September 2002): 677–689.

Public Service Ad by Google. "Childhood Depression." *Fighting Depression*. 2006 http:www.fightingdepression.couk/Fighting-depression/childhood-depression.asp (26, January 2006).

Robiner, David. "ADHD and Depression." *Focus Adolescent Services*. 2000, http:// www.focusas.com/ADHD-Depression.html (26, January 2006).

Rogers, Carl R. "Characteristics of a Helping Relationship." *American Personnel and Guidance* Journal 37, no.1 (1958): 6–16.

Rogers, Carl R. "The Necessary and Sufficient Conditions of Therapeutic Personality Change." *Journal of Consulting Psychology* 21, no.2 (1957): 459–461.

Shealy, C.N. "From Boys Town to Oliver Twist: Separating Fact From Fiction in Welfare Reform and Out-of-Home Placements of Children and Youth." *American Psychologist* 50, no.8 (August 1995): 565–580.

Weiss, Lynn. *Attention Deficit Disorder in Adults*. Lanham, MD: Taylor Trade Publishing, 2005.